PARTY *Punches*

PUNCH RECIPES
FROM AROUND THE WORLD

Tim Page
and
Marianne Page Smith

with Amy Charlene Reed

The Overmountain Press
JOHNSON CITY, TENNESSEE

Book design by Bill May Jr.

This book includes new recipes, along with some of the
best recipes originally published in *Party Punches*
by Page Press and Associates, Incorporated, in 1986.

ISBN 1-57072-233-1
Copyright © 2004 by Tim Page and Marianne Page Smith
Printed in the United States of America
All Rights Reserved

1 2 3 4 5 6 7 8 9 0

In memory of

Evelyn Page

Acknowledgments

We wish to thank the many people who have contributed to this book over the past decades for their enthusiasm and for their encouragement.

For their support, special thanks goes to Mrs. John Powell, former librarian at the Lawson McGhee Library in Knoxville, Tennessee; Ellen Monroe, formerly of the Home Service Division of the Knoxville Utilities Board; Ken Stilts of Nashville, Tennessee; Mrs. John C. Lunsford, mother of the late Evelyn Page; Fay and Jim Picquet of Sun Graphics in Oak Ridge, Tennessee; Jim England of the Last Lap in Knoxville, Tennessee; Mary Espenshade of Knoxville, Tennessee; Ernie and Norma Owens of Owens Construction in Knoxville, Tennessee; Noel Smith of Knoxville, Tennessee; and Mr. and Mrs. Jim Yancy of Starkville, Mississippi.

For recipes shared with us, special thanks goes to the staff of the embassies of nations around the world, state governors' offices and mansions, and countless others who shared with us their punch creations, many of which had never before been published. We especially thank Jay Kenneth Katzen, David Norman, George A. Morgan, Robert E. Lamb, James P. Sullivan, Geoffrey W. Lewis, Andrew V. Corry, S. MacLeod Robertson, Louise T. Farnus, Claire F. Chandler, Ruth A. McLendon, Jean Jacques Hediger, Dorothy J. Boland, Franz H. Misch, John J. Hagemann, Robert C. Strong, Elizabeth Mattson, E. Russell Linch, Henry E. Stebbins, James W. Shinn, Marion E. Brown, Dorothy Dingman, Paul W. Deibel, Mrs. Graham Martin, Katherine E. White, J. Kajeckas, Tina J. C. Ferringa, H. Wilcox, Hubert L. Yates, Bess Abell, Maxine H. Hartin, Mrs. George Wallace, William A. Egan, Julia A. Goddard, Orval F. Faubus, Eileen A. Dillon, Mrs. John A. Love, Teresa M. Messick, Mrs. Haydon Burns, Mrs. Carl E. Sanders, Leslie A. Holland, Mrs. William H. Avery, Edward T. Breathitt, Mrs. John J. McKeithen, Mrs. Esther L. Shaw, Ann Cain, Mrs. John A. Volpe, Mrs. George Romney, Mrs. Karl F. Rolvaag, Mrs. Warren E. Hearnes, Mrs. Elsie Jones, Mrs. Frank B. Morrison, Grant Sawyer, Mrs. Jack M. Campbell, Dan K. Moore, Mrs. William L. Guy, James A. Rhodes, Mrs. Robert E. McNair, Mrs. Frank G. Clement, John J. Daley, V. Francis Walters, Mrs. Daniel J. Evans, Mrs. Hulett C. Smith, Warren P. Knowles, and Mrs. Clifford P. Hansen.

Table of *Contents*

Introduction

The idea for this book began in my father's college days in the 1950s when his fraternity at East Tennessee State University was suddenly restricted from serving alcohol just days before a large party was planned. Daddy, who was in charge of providing the beverage, hurriedly began searching for a non-alcoholic punch recipe that would be flavorful enough to interest his fraternity friends and their dates.

To his dismay, the only punch recipes to be found in cookbooks were bland and uninteresting. Then one of his friends, Thayer Smith, mentioned that his family's cook made a terrific punch that the cook had learned while serving at the Tennessee Governor's Mansion in Nashville. The young men called the cook, took down details on how to make the punch, and prepared it for the party.

"It was an instant success," Daddy recalls. "I knew the recipe was special when college-aged guys began asking me if they could buy it bottled somewhere. I don't think that all of them realized at the time that it didn't have any alcohol in it."

Ever an entrepreneur, he began researching the idea of publishing a cookbook devoted to punch and other festive party drinks. The response he received was overwhelming. "I began contacting anyone I could think of who might frequently serve punch," he said, "including embassies around the world, governors' offices, the White House. Punch recipes began pouring in from all over, some with notes mentioning that the recipes had never before been written down."

Libraries encouraged him as well. One librarian in particular implored him to go through with the project. She said, "I can't tell you how many brides and their mothers come to the library and look through all the cookbooks, comparing what few punch recipes they can find. It would be wonderful to have a comprehensive collection in one book."

When Daddy and my late mother married in 1962, she became caught up in the excitement of the project as well. A devout Christian, Mama ardently believed that this book could serve an important purpose by offering festive beverages that allowed people to celebrate special events without serving alcoholic drinks.

When the first edition of this book was published in 1986, it was a tremendous success. The First Lady of Tennessee at the time, Mrs. Lamar

Alexander, sent copies of the book as gifts to every governor's wife in the United States. Ken Stilts, who represented country music stars Wynonna and Naomi Judd, purchased 100 copies of the book to give as Christmas presents. Orders for the book came in from around the world, from the Middle East to Europe to Asia.

We've come to realize that this book serves two roles. It is a recipe book of party beverages for families today to use at festive celebrations, and it also is the world's only historic record of punches.

At last count, we had recorded a total of more than 2,000 recipes, with around 300 of our favorite nonalcoholic punches and other party beverages featured in this edition.

Generations of families around the globe have used the recipes presented here for their celebrations for decades, even centuries in some cases. Our hope is that your family will use these recipes for special events in your life just as our family has, beginning with my father's first punch nearly 50 years ago.

Marianne Page Smith

Measurement Equivalence Chart

a dash	= 1/8 teaspoon
60 drops	= 1 teaspoon
3 teaspoons	= 1 tablespoon
2 tablespoons	= 1 ounce
8 ounces	= 1 cup
2 cups	= 1 pint
2 pints	= 1 quart
4 quarts	= 1 gallon
#300 can commercial canned goods	= 2 cups
#2 can commercial canned goods	= 2-1/2 cups
#2-1/2 can commercial canned goods	= 3-1/2 cups
#10 can commercial canned goods	= 13 cups

TOP TEN
All-time Favorites

Of the more than 2,000 recipes for punches and other party beverages that our family has collected from all corners of the world, we have highlighted here our top ten all-time favorites. Narrowing our selection down to just a handful of recipes was difficult, and we encourage you to experiment with other recipes in the book to find your own personal favorites.

Tennessee Governor's Punch

Still our family's favorite punch after all these years, this is the recipe that launched the idea for this cookbook nearly half a century ago. Like many of the other recipes in our collection, this one had never before been published until we recorded it in our first edition. In fact, the cook who gave the verbal instructions on how to prepare this punch said he had never seen the recipe written down, even in the kitchen of the Tennessee Governor's Mansion in Nashville, where he learned to make it.

8 cups water
3 cinnamon sticks
2 cups sugar
1 twelve-ounce can orange juice concentrate
12-14 fresh lemons
1 forty-six-ounce can unsweetened pineapple juice
1 large bottle ginger ale, chilled
1 bottle long-stem maraschino cherries
3-6 oranges, sliced

Boil water and cinnamon sticks until water begins to turn red (about 10 minutes). Remove cinnamon sticks and add sugar, mix well. Boil for five more minutes. Remove from heat.

Prepare orange juice from concentrate, following label instructions. Squeeze juice from fresh lemons, making approximately 1-1/2 cups juice.

Mix sugar syrup, orange juice, pineapple juice, and 1 cup of lemon juice (reserve remaining half cup). Chill well.

Just before serving, mix punch concentrate with ginger ale.

Taste, adding remaining half cup of lemon juice and additional sugar as needed.

Garnish with maraschino cherries and orange slices.

Serves 35-40.

Wedding Ring Punch

This was my late mother's favorite punch because of its striking presentation. When the first edition of this book was published, Mama served this punch at a book-signing event at Proffitt's department store in Knoxville, Tennessee, in the summer of 1986. As shoppers began sampling the punch, there was a stampede for the cookbooks. Daddy, who was standing next to her handling sales, could hardly keep up with the transactions, at one point selling 30 books in 27 minutes.

10 canned apricot halves
1 cup seedless grapes
1/2 cup boiling water
cold water
2 six-ounce cans frozen limeade concentrate
2 six-ounce cans frozen lemonade concentrate
2 cans (1 pint 2 ounces each) unsweetened grapefruit juice, chilled
2 cans (1 pint 2 ounces each) pineapple juice, chilled
3-1/2 quarts crushed ice
3 quarts ginger ale, chilled

Make decorative wreath day before:
Make frozen punch wreath by arranging apricot halves and grapes in bottom of 1-1/4 quart ring mold. Add just enough boiling water to cover fruit. Freeze until solid. Then fill mold to top with cold water. Freeze solid.

Just before serving:
Blend undiluted concentrates with grapefruit juice, pineapple juice, and crushed ice in punch bowl.

Remove ring mold from freezer and place in shallow hot water briefly. Then unmold the ice wreath and set on top of the punch. Pour ginger ale into punch bowl.

Serves about 50.

MOCK CHAMPAGNE PUNCH

This elegant punch is similar in color to champagne and is an excellent choice for formal adult gatherings.

6 cups water
6 cups sugar
2 quarts fresh grapefruit juice, chilled
6 quarts ginger ale, chilled
1 block of ice

Boil water and sugar in saucepan for 5 minutes, stirring until sugar is dissolved. Cool. Mix with grapefruit juice. Chill well. Just before serving, pour over ice and add ginger ale.
Serves 60.

LADY BIRD JOHNSON'S ORANGE PUNCH

This recipe was shared with us by Bess Abell, former social secretary for the White House during President Lyndon B. Johnson's administration in the 1960s. She said that this punch was a family favorite of Lady Bird Johnson's.

1 gallon orange juice
1 quart lemon juice
1 quart pineapple juice
1 gallon water
2 quarts ginger ale
sugar (typically about 1 cup)

Mix fruit juices and water, then chill overnight. Just before serving, pour into a large bowl with a block of ice in the center. Add ginger ale. Add sugar to taste. Stir.

Note: Although the original recipe calls for sugar to be added straight into the punch, the flavor can be enhanced by making a sugar syrup—boil 1-1/2 cups sugar and 3/4 cup of water for five minutes—and then adding it to taste.

Serves 50.

TENNESSEE ORANGE JULEP

As delicious and refreshing as it is quick and easy, this is simple enough to prepare at a tailgate party during football season. For best results, keep ingredients well chilled.

1 pint orange sherbet
1 quart ginger ale, chilled
fresh mint
orange slices
maraschino cherries

Divide orange sherbet equally in five to six glasses and fill with ginger ale. Stir lightly and garnish with sprigs of mint, orange slices, and cherries. Serve immediately.

For a richer, creamier version, try "Orange Slush Punch" (recipe on page 75).

Serves 5-6.

Cassie's Slushie Cherry Punch

Another of our family favorites, this can be made up ahead and then served as needed, whether for one person or a whole family.

My mother-in-law, Bobbie Smith, introduced me to this punch during my college days, when my husband and I often studied together in the evenings. During our marathon study sessions, she often refreshed us with two glasses of this icy, delicious punch served with a bowl of hot, buttered popcorn.

1 large box cherry-flavored gelatin mix (Jell-O)
water
2 cinnamon sticks
12 lemons
2 large cans pineapple juice
4 cups sugar
1 pint tea
2 liters lemon-lime soft drink or ginger ale

Bring water to a boil, according to directions on gelatin box. Remove from heat and add gelatin mix and cinnamon sticks. Stir until gelatin dissolves. Add enough water to make one gallon.

Squeeze lemons, making 1/2 cup to 2/3 cup juice.

Add fruit juices, sugar, and tea to gelatin mixture, making punch concentrate.

Freeze punch concentrate in ice-cube trays until frozen solid. Store in sealed plastic bag in freezer.

To serve, fill tall glasses with cubes of frozen punch concentrate. Fill with lemon-lime carbonated beverage or ginger ale. Crush punch concentrate cubes with fork.

Serve with iced teaspoons.

Serves about 40.

Classic Fruit Punch

This traditional recipe includes the three key aspects to a flavorful punch—a basic sugar syrup, a variety of fruit juices, and tea to harmonize the flavor.

1-1/8 cups water
2-1/4 cups sugar
2 cups strawberry jelly, thinned
1 cup strong tea
2 cups orange juice, fresh-squeezed
1 cup lemon juice, fresh-squeezed
1 cup pineapple juice, canned
1 cup white grape juice, bottled
1 quart carbonated water, chilled
1 cup maraschino cherries with juice

Mix water and sugar in saucepan over medium-high heat, stirring until sugar is dissolved. Boil for 5 minutes. Set aside 1/4 cup syrup mixture.

In bowl, blend 2 cups strawberry jelly with about 1/4 cup of water to thin.

In large pitcher, mix together sugar syrup, jelly, tea, orange juice, lemon juice, pineapple juice, and grape juice to make punch concentrate. Chill well (best if refrigerated overnight to let flavors blend).

Just before serving, add enough ice water to make a total of 1-1/2 gallons. Add carbonated water and cherries (including cherry juice).

If punch needs more sweetener, add reserved syrup mixture.

Serves about 50.

Dinner Punch

For adult gatherings such as dinner parties, this tea-flavored punch is one of our favorites.

1-1/2 cups sugar
1-1/2 cups water
4 cups hot, strong tea
6 tablespoons chopped mint
1-1/2 cups lemon juice
2-1/2 cups orange juice
1 cup grapefruit juice
1/4 cup lime juice
1/2 teaspoon salt
rind of 3 cucumbers, cut into long strips
7-1/2 cups white grape juice
4 twelve-ounce bottles ginger ale, chilled
2 twelve-ounce bottles sparkling water, chilled
ice
orange slices
lemon slices
sprigs of mint

Boil sugar and water together for 5 minutes. Remove from heat.
Pour hot tea over chopped mint in large pot, let stand several minutes.
Add sugar syrup, lemon juice, orange juice, grapefruit juice, lime juice, salt, and cucumber rind.
Let stand until cool. Strain and chill.
Just before serving, add grape juice, ginger ale, and sparkling water.
Pour over ice and garnish with orange and lemon slices and mint sprigs.
Serves 25.

Watermelon Sharbat

Children, especially, enjoy making and serving this unusual punch recipe, which originated in Pakistan and uses the watermelon shell as the punch bowl. Have the watermelon well chilled before beginning.

seedless watermelon (about 5 pounds), chilled
1 lime
1/2 pound sugar
red food coloring, liquid
2 liters ginger ale, chilled
dash of salt

Preferably working on an outdoor picnic table, slice a thin strip off the bottom of the watermelon to help stabilize it as you work, being careful not to puncture the rind. Carve a 6-inch (or larger) square hole in the top center of the watermelon, remove cut section, and set aside in a clean bowl.

With clean hands, use a large serving fork or potato masher to reach inside the watermelon and mash the inner red pulp into small bits, scraping the inner shell as needed to loosen all pulp.

(Alternately, for a smoother drink, the pulp can be scooped out with a wide, short cup into a bowl, processed in a blender, strained, and then poured back into the watermelon shell.)

Squeeze juice from lime. Mix lime juice, sugar, and melon juices inside melon shell, stirring well. Plug cut piece back into opening to close melon. Chill for about 1 hour.

Before serving, remove plug and mix well with fork. If desired, add a few drops of red food coloring to intensify color.

Ladle mixture from the watermelon shell into glasses (children enjoy doing this step themselves), filling glasses halfway. Fill remainder of glass with ginger ale. Add a dash of salt to each glass. Stir lightly and serve.

Color-Coordinated Punch

To color-coordinate a punch with a specific decorating scheme, this delicious recipe works well. The gelatin dessert mix selected determines the color (cherry for red punch, lemon for yellow punch, etc.).

3 lemons, juiced
1 large (6 ounce) box gelatin mix (Jell-O)
1-1/2 cups sugar
1 cup hot water
2 quarts water
1 quart ginger ale, chilled
crushed ice

Squeeze juice from lemons, set aside. Mix gelatin and sugar in hot water, stirring until dissolved. Immediately add lemon juice and water to prevent gelatin from congealing.

Just before serving, add ginger ale to punch. Serve in glasses filled with crushed ice.

Serves 15.

SECRETS TO A Perfect Punch

PREPARING

These tips will enhance the flavor of nearly any punch.

Use sugar syrup. For the best sweetener, use a sugar syrup to intensify the flavor of the punch, rather than mixing dry sugar directly with the fruit juices. To make a basic sugar syrup, boil equal parts sugar and water for five to ten minutes, stirring until the sugar is dissolved. Sugar syrup can be made ahead and stored in the refrigerator.

Balance sweet and sour. When blending fruit juices, be sure to include a tart juice such as lemon, lime, or rhubarb, which gives the necessary acidity.

Chill well. Punch must be served very cold—almost icy—to be its most appetizing. The night before making the punch, refrigerate all liquid ingredients. When serving, keep the punch cold by using ice blocks, frozen blocks of punch, or by filling the punch bowl with only a portion of the punch at a time, keeping the remainder well chilled until needed.

Fresh-squeeze citrus juices. For best flavor, squeeze juice from fresh oranges and lemons if time permits. Canned or bottled juices work well for other fruits such as pineapples and peaches.

Preserve carbonation. Wait until just before serving time to add carbonated beverages, such as ginger ale, to avoid losing carbonation.

Include tea. A cup or so of tea added to any fruit punch will help harmonize the flavors of the fruit juices.

SERVING

Many times punch is not only the main beverage at a celebration but also serves as a centerpiece on the serving table. Creative garnishes can add to a festive atmosphere and sometimes serve the dual role of helping keep the punch well chilled.

Festive ice floats. Pour a thin layer (about 1/4 inch) of boiled water (which freezes more clearly than cold tap water) into a ring mold or, to make a traditional ice block, into a rectangular or round cake pan. Carefully place garnishes such as maraschino cherries, mint leaves, or sliced oranges and lemons in the water and freeze solid. Then fill pan near to brim with cold water and freeze. At serving time, remove from freezer and set in a shallow pan of very hot water for about 30 seconds. Remove ice block from pan and float on top of punch in punch bowl.

Two of our favorite ice floats are the rosebud ring featured in "Punch Served at the Nevada Executive Mansion" and the fruit ice wreath in "Wedding Ring Punch."

Garnished ice cubes. Pour boiled water into ice-cube tray, filling about half full. Freeze. Place one of the following in each cube: red or green maraschino cherries, mint leaves, small flowers, or small berries. Finish filling tray with water and freeze again. For an added effect, use water tinted with cherry juice, grenadine, or food coloring.

Icy full-strength punch. The last cup of punch should be as flavorful as the first. To keep punch chilled without diluting it, freeze about a fourth of the punch in ice-cube trays or in a cake pan and add to the punch bowl at serving time.

Frosted and candied fruit. For frosted fruit, place unpeeled fruit on a tray and freeze, uncovered, for about three hours. At serving time, remove from freezer and place in punch bowl at once. As soon as the room-temperature air strikes the fruit, frosted coating will appear.

Candied apples make a delightful garnish for an autumn punch or cider. See "Floating Apple Wassail" for instructions.

Sugar-rimmed glasses. Dip the rim of each glass into lemon juice, water, or a beaten egg white, and then into sugar. Chill the glasses in the refrigerator to harden the sugar.

Floral decorations. Flowers that complement the color of the punch can be strung together with wire to make a wreath to fasten around the rim of the punch bowl.

Serving size: Most punch cups will hold a four-ounce serving.

PUNCHES FROM

Around THE World

This historic collection of punch recipes from around the world is the result of nearly half a century of research. Many of the recipes we recorded had been used for generations but had never before been written down.

Punch originated in the 7th century in Persia, an ancient empire that included parts of present-day Iran and Afghanistan. When Islamic Arabs conquered Persia in A.D. 641, the drinking of alcohol was forbidden. Cool, fruit-based drinks came into general use as a substitute.

Punch recipes soon spread to India, where the word punch *in the Hindustani language means "five" for its five basic ingredients: spirit, water, sugar, lime or other fruit juices, and spices. When the British occupied India in the 18th century, they were taken with the taste and cooling qualities of punch and began to serve it throughout the empire. Punch then became popular in the United States, especially in the South.*

While we have collected punch recipes from nearly every country on earth, this edition features those that exemplify the nonalcoholic properties of the original punch concept.

GABON: CAFÉ LEIGEOISE

2 quarts cold, strong coffee
3 cups light cream
1/2 cup sugar
2 teaspoons vanilla
1 bar bittersweet chocolate
1-1/2 quarts coffee ice cream
whipped cream

In a large bowl, combine coffee, 1 cup cream (reserve remaining 2 cups), sugar, and vanilla.

Stir until the sugar is dissolved and mixture is well blended. Chill in refrigerator two hours or overnight.

Whip remaining 2 cups of cream until peaks form, adding sugar to taste. Grate chocolate and set aside for garnish.

Immediately prior to serving, pour coffee mixture over ice cream in large punch bowl. Top with whipped cream, and then sprinkle lightly with grated chocolate.

If served in individual tall glasses, this also makes an excellent dessert.

Makes 16 small servings, 8 large.

Ivory Coast: Fruit Punch

1 quart pineapple juice
6 oranges
2 lemons
1 pint sparkling water
ice

Squeeze juice from oranges (juice should equal 1-1/2 cups). Squeeze juice from lemons (juice should equal 2 tablespoons). Mix all fruit juices and then chill.

Just before serving, pour fruit juice mixture over ice and add sparkling water.

Serves 8.

Liberia: Pineapple-Orange Punch

6 cups pineapple juice
3 cups orange juice
1 cup sugar cane juice (or ginger ale)

Mix juices and chill well. Before serving pour ingredients over ice in serving bowl and then add ginger ale.

Serves 6.

Mauritania: Zreeg

Geoffrey W. Lewis, former staff member of the U.S. Embassy in Mauritania in western Africa, recorded this traditional recipe. Mr. Lewis noted that because Mauritania is a Muslim country, alcohol is not widely consumed. Traditionally, the most common drinks have been tea and milk-based drinks.

1 gallon camel's milk
cow's urine
sugar

Place camel's milk in goatskin sack. Wet the outside of sack with cow's urine twice during a 24-hour period. Before serving, shake vigorously then pour into gourd for drinking. Sugar may be added to taste.

Sierra Leone: Mint Punch

12 sprigs mint
1 cup boiling hot water
1 cup currant jelly
1 cup cold water
1/2 cup lemon juice
3 cups orange juice
1 bottle ginger ale
ice

Crush mint in a bowl and add boiling water and currant jelly. When jelly is melted, add cold water. When mixture is cool enough to handle, strain into punch bowl. Add fruit juices and block of ice. Just before serving, pour in ginger ale.
Serves 8.

South Africa: Nonalcoholic Punch

1/2 gallon orange juice
2 pints fresh pineapple juice
8 ounces guava juice
8 ounces granadilla (passion fruit) juice
1 pineapple, diced
2 apples, diced
2 guavas, diced
4 granadillas, diced
sprig of mint
12 cherries, diced

Mix first eight ingredients together and chill well. Before serving, add mint sprigs and cherries for garnish.
Serves 10.

Tunisia: Mint Tea

2 cups sugar
1/2 cup water
grated rind of 1 orange
6 glasses of very strong tea
6 oranges, juiced
18 sprigs of mint
2 oranges, thinly sliced
crushed ice

Boil sugar, water, and orange rind in saucepan for 5 minutes, then remove from heat. Crush six mint sprigs and add to mixture. Let cool.

In separate pitcher, mix tea and orange juice.

Half fill tall glasses with crushed ice. Pour tea mixture over ice and sweeten to taste with mint syrup. For garnish, add a sprig of mint and a slice of orange to each glass.
Serves 12.

Zaire: Pineapple Punch

1 pineapple (fresh, not canned)
5 cups sugar
5 cups water
24 lemons
24 oranges
10 cups strong, hot tea
2 quarts carbonated water
canned cherries
ice

Core and peel pineapple. Mince pineapple pulp in a food processor (or finely chop the pulp into small pieces and then mash with a fork or potato masher). Put pulp in medium-sized saucepan with sugar and water. Bring to a boil, then simmer about 15 minutes or until pulp looks nearly clear.

While syrup mixture is simmering, squeeze the juice from lemons and oranges. When syrup mixture is done, let it cool before adding tea and juice from oranges and lemons.

At serving time, pour mixture over ice in serving bowl, then add carbonated water. Taste for sweetness, adding sugar if needed. For extra flavor and color, add a can of red cherries.

Serves 20.

Afghanistan: Spring Party Punch

> 1 quart boiling water
> 1-1/2 teaspoons black tea
> 5 whole cloves
> 1 cup orange juice
> 1 quart lime juice
> 1/2 cup lemon juice
> 1/2 cup liquid honey
> 1 cup cold water
> crushed ice
> orange, cherry, or mint garnish

In saucepan, pour boiling water over tea and cloves. Cover and let steep for 5 minutes, then strain.

Fill glasses with crushed ice. In a pitcher, combine tea mixture with other ingredients and pour into glasses. Garnish with thin orange slices, red cherries, or mint leaves.

Serves 12.

Pakistan: Mango Sharbat

This drink is often served as an appetizer before lunch and is most popular during the sultry mango season in Pakistan.

> 1 pound raw mangoes
> 1/2 pound sugar
> water

Steam mangoes until tender. Cool and then peel. Place in a pint of cool water and mash into a fine paste. Add sugar, mixing well.

Add another pint of water, stir well, and place in refrigerator until chilled.

Iran: Sekanjabin

1 pound sugar
3 cups water
1 cup vinegar
2 pounds fresh mint
ice

Mix sugar and water in large saucepan, bring to a boil. Boil and stir for 5 minutes. Turn off heat, add vinegar and mint (including stems), cover saucepan with lid.

On top of saucepan lid, place a container of cool water to prevent the escape of the steam and "essence" of the drink, as well as to speed the cooling.

To serve, pour over ice in glasses, adding water to taste.

Note: There are two variables in this recipe. Depending on whether one likes the drink sweet or sour, the ratio of vinegar and sugar can be adjusted. Also, if a thicker concentrate is desired, the boiling time can be extended.

Iran: Paludeh Sib (Apple Punch)

This is a typical Persian punch made from grated fresh fruit and rose water. Rose water, which is water scented with oil of roses, is a key ingredient and can be obtained in the Greek food section of specialty grocery stores.

4 medium apples
2 tablespoons lemon juice
5 tablespoons powdered sugar
2 teaspoons rose water
4 cups crushed ice

Peel the apples and grate them. Sprinkle the grated apples with lemon juice to prevent darkening.

Add sugar and rose water to apple mixture and stir lightly. Refrigerate for three hours. About 10 minutes before serving, add crushed ice. More rose water can be added to taste.

Serves 3-4.

Lebanon: Pineapple Punch

1 large can pineapple juice
8 bottles 7-Up or Sprite
pineapple slices

Chill ingredients well. Just before serving, combine pineapple juice and soft drink. Add pineapple slices for garnish.

Iraq: Fruit Punch

1 cup water
2 cups sugar
1 cup strong hot tea
2 cups fruit syrup (or grenadine)
1 cup lemon juice
2 cups orange juice (unsweetened)
2 cups pineapple juice (unsweetened)
ice water
1 quart soda water
1 cup maraschino cherries (optional)

Combine 1 cup water and sugar in saucepan; boil 5 minutes to make basic sugar syrup. Remove from heat and add tea, fruit syrup or grenadine, and fruit juices to sugar syrup. Let stand 30 minutes or more to cool.

Before serving, add ice water to make a total of 1-1/2 gallons. Add 1 quart soda water and cherries.

Serves 50.

Syria: Tamarind Drink

The fruit or pod of the tropical tamarind tree has an acid pulp used for preserves and a cooling, laxative drink.

12 tamarind sticks
water
sugar
ice

Night before: Fill four glasses with water. Place three tamarind sticks in each glass. Let stand overnight.
Before serving: Strain liquid. Add sugar and ice to taste.
Serves 4.

Syria: Apricot Punch

dried apricots
water
sugar

Soak dried apricots in water until they are enlarged. Remove apricots from liquid, add sugar to taste. Chill before serving.

Syria: Liquorice Punch

liquorice roots
water

Cut liquorice roots into pieces, wrap in thin, white, cotton fabric, and place in water. Let stand overnight. When the water becomes black, strain liquid to remove roots and any loose particles. Add more water until the taste is pleasant. Serve cold.

BURMA: PLUM PUNCH

This Burmese recipe calls for zi-thi, a type of plum native to Burma, but red plums or sour red cherries available in the United States can be substituted.

red plums or sour red cherries
water
sugar
ice
carbonated water
limes, sliced

Night before: Wash plums thoroughly, then place in a very large saucepan. Add water until tops of plums are covered by an inch of water. (To avoid overboiling, pan should be not more than half full.)

Cook at medium heat until the fruit is completely tender. Remove from heat, drain water, and mash the plums to a pulp. Pour the pulp into a clean muslin bag and hang over a bowl to drip overnight, as for a jelly, without pressing.

Next day: Discard remains in muslin bag. Measure pulp liquid in bowl, and then measure an equal amount of sugar, setting sugar aside in separate bowl.

Pour pulp liquid into a saucepan; bring to a boil. Skim boiling liquid until it is quite clear. Add sugar, boil for 20 minutes. When cool, strain.

To serve, fill glasses with crushed ice. Fill glasses with carbonated water, adding 2 tablespoons of the syrup for each glass.

Remaining syrup can be stored in refrigerator for several days.

Sri Lanka: Ceylon Punch

1-1/4 cups water
1-1/4 cups sugar
2-1/2 cups strong hot tea
2-1/2 cups strawberry juice
6 limes, juiced
7 oranges, juiced
1 cup crushed pineapple
cold water
1 cup maraschino cherries and juice
1 quart carbonated water

Boil water and sugar for 10 minutes. Add freshly made hot tea. Cool, then add fruit juices and pineapple. Chill ingredients for 1 hour. Add sufficient water to make a total of 4 quarts of liquid.

Just before serving, add cherries (including juice) and carbonated water. Pour over large block of ice in punch bowl.

India: Mango Fool

6 medium-sized mangoes (if large, use 3)
crushed ice
1 cup sugar (or sugar to taste; salt and pepper may be used
    instead of sugar if preferred)
milk

Bake mangoes over coals until the pulp can be removed from the seed. (Alternately, mangoes can be boiled until tender.) Remove pulp and add crushed ice to make a thick consistency. Add sugar (or salt and pepper if desired). If the mixture is too sour, sweeten with additional sugar according to taste.

To serve, half fill glasses with the mango liquid and then add milk.

Note: Milk helps to lessen the sourness of raw mango, in which case less sugar can be used.

Indonesia: Dawet (Tear Drops)

2 cups water
1 cup rice flour
1/2 cup water
2 cups coconut milk (juice), preferably of a young coconut
1 teaspoon vanilla flavoring
1/4 teaspoon salt
1/2 cup sugar

Mix 2 cups of water and rice flour in saucepan, stirring until well blended. Heat over medium heat until boiling, stirring constantly.

Holding sieve over a bowl filled with 1/2 cup of water, pour flour mixture into sieve. With a wooden spoon or spatula, force flour mixture through sieve and into bowl of water. Pressed flour mixture should resemble teardrops.

Mix coconut milk, vanilla flavoring, salt, and sugar in separate saucepan. Over medium heat, stir constantly and bring to a boil. Remove from heat. Chill both mixtures.

To serve, fill glasses with crushed ice, coconut mixture, and teardrop mixture.

JAPAN: FRUIT PUNCH

1 cup sugar
2 cups water
30 ounces lemon juice
12 ounces orange juice concentrate
2 boxes frozen whole strawberries
2 quarts ginger ale
2 quarts sparkling water
2 pints sherbet
ice cubes (or block of ice)

Boil sugar and water for 5 minutes to make sugar syrup. Remove from heat and cool. When cooled, add lemon juice and orange juice concentrate. Refrigerate until serving time.

Before serving, partially thaw strawberries. Add strawberries to chilled mixture and stir. Pour mixture over ice in serving bowl. Add ginger ale and sparkling water. Using melon scoop or small ice cream scoop, scoop out small balls of sherbet and add to punch.

Serves 40.

THAILAND: MINT FRUIT PUNCH

1-3/4 cups sugar
1 cup chopped mint
4 cups water
1 cup pineapple juice
1/2 cup lime juice
2-1/2 cups orange juice
ice cold water
ginger ale
orange slices and fresh mint garnish

Boil sugar, mint leaves, and water for five minutes. Remove from heat, strain, and cool. Add fruit juices. Dilute to taste with ice water and ginger ale. Serve over crushed ice. Garnish with orange slices and fresh mint.

Nepal: Thon (or Chhang)

The first edition of this book, printed in 1986, marked the first time this age-old recipe had been published, although it has since been published in a major geographic magazine.

The art of chhang-making has been highly developed through centuries by the Newars in Kathmandu. Almost every Newar woman knows how to prepare the drink. To prevent the spirits of the dead from spoiling the cooked rice during the three- to four-day process, Newars usually add a piece of charcoal and a chili pepper.

In Newari, this drink is called *thon*, and the terms given here for ingredients and utensils are Newari. The Nepali word for this drink is *jand*, and the Sherpa name is *chhang*.

Ingredients:
    rice (or corn or millet)
    manapu (yeast), made of wheat or rice
    water

Utensils:
    phosi—a copper vessel, capacity 2 gallons
    potasi—an earthen pot with holes in the bottom
    bhalincha—a bamboo dish to fit the potasi and stop the holes
    bhega—an earthen tub
    koncha—an earthen pot
    ba—a bamboo strainer

Process:
    1. Take 4 pounds of rice.
    2. Soak rice in water for about 8 hours.
    3. Strain the water.
    4. Fill the phosi with 1 gallon of water; bring to a boil.
    5. Place the potasi on the phosi. Use a wet cloth around the phosi to prevent the steam from coming out.
    6. Place the bhalincha in the potasi, so as to stop the holes.
    7. Pour the rice into the potasi.
    8. Cover the potasi with the bhega.
    9. Build up the fire until drops of steam appear outside the bhega.

10. Remove the bhega.

11. Take out the rice, which will be half-cooked.

12. Wash the rice in cold water.

13. Strain the water from the rice.

14. Refill the potasi with the rice.

15. Replace the bhega.

16. Build up the fire until drops of steam appear outside the bhega.

17. Take out the rice, now fully cooked.

18. Spread the rice on a cleanly swept floor.

19. Take a tablespoon of manapu.

20. Mix the manapu thoroughly with the rice—in winter, when the rice is still warm; during summer, when the rice has cooled.

21. Keep the rice in a koncha.

22. Close the mouth of the koncha tightly, and keep the koncha covered with straw or wrapped up in old clothes for 3 to 4 days. On the third day, the rice gives a sweet smell and is greenish with mold.

23. For drinking on the fourth day, take out a pound of the rice. Now it is called *poka*.

24. Add 2 pounds of cold water, stir and allow it to stand about 8 hours.

25. Strain. The clear, sweet thon is now ready to drink.

Philippines: Calamansi Punch

This punch is made from the calamansi, a small, acidic, loose-skinned citrus fruit that is native to the Philippines.

3 cups sugar
1-1/2 cups water
1/2 cup calamansi juice
2 cups pineapple juice
3/4 cup orange juice
maraschino cherries

Mix sugar and water together in saucepan over medium-high heat, stirring until sugar is dissolved. Boil for five minutes. Cool.

Mix sugar syrup with juices. Chill well, serving in glasses half filled with crushed ice. Garnish with maraschino cherries.

Philippines: Mango Punch

8 ounces mango juice
1 quart ginger ale
1 cup mango, scooped and diced

Chill ingredients well. To serve, pour mango juice and ginger ale over ice in punch bowl. Add a little sugar if needed. Add the diced mango.

Philippines: Tea Punch

2 teaspoons tea
1-1/4 cups boiling water
1 cup sugar
3/4 cup orange juice
1/3 cup lemon juice
1 pint ginger ale
1 pint soda water
orange slices

Make tea infusion by pouring boiling water over tea. Add sugar. As soon as sugar dissolves, add fruit juices. Strain into punch bowl over a large piece of ice. Just before serving, add ginger ale and soda water, garnishing with orange slices.

PHILIPPINES: GUWAYABANO-DUHAT PUNCH

3 cups soursop (guwayabano) juice
3 tablespoons duhat juice
1 cup sugar
3 cups water

Mix ingredients and stir until sugar is dissolved. Pour over crushed ice and serve.

PHILIPPINES: FRUIT PUNCH

4 cups sugar
2 cups water
1-1/2 teaspoons tea
1 cup boiling water
1 cup lemon juice or calamansi juice
1/2 cup crushed pineapple
3 oranges, sliced
4 quarts ice water

Mix sugar and water together in saucepan over medium-high heat, stirring until sugar is dissolved. In separate saucepan, add tea to 1 cup boiling water. Mix together sugar syrup, tea infusion, juices, and fruit. Chill well.
To serve, pour over a block of ice in punch bowl and add ice water.
Serves 20.

Denmark: Red Currant Punch for Those Who Must Drive

1/2 cup currant jelly
2 cups ice water
1/2 cup lemon juice
1/2 cup orange juice
1 pint ginger ale
orange slices

Using an egg whisk or blender, whisk jelly and juices with ice water. Just before serving, add ginger ale and pour over ice in punch bowl. Garnish with slices of orange.

Iceland: Grape-Lemonade Punch

2 cans lemonade concentrate
2 cans grape juice concentrate
2 liters ginger ale, chilled
2 lemons, thinly sliced

Prepare lemonade and grape juice as packages indicate. Add ginger ale. Float lemon slices on top of punch.
Serves 10.

Lithuania: Cranberry and Ginger Ale

1 pint cranberry juice
2 liters ginger ale
mint sprigs

Mix cranberry juice and ginger ale just before serving. Place a sprig of fresh mint in each cup.

Netherlands: Punch Bowl of Strawberries

2 pounds strawberries
1/2 pound soft (fine) sugar
1 bottle cider
lemon juice
1 bottle soda water

Wash strawberries in water, then cut each strawberry in half. In bowl, mix strawberries and sugar. Let stand three hours or more. Add cider and as much of the lemon juice as desired until the punch has a refreshing taste. Cover bowl and chill well. Just before serving add soda water.

AUSTRALIA: SPICED PINEAPPLE PUNCH

1-1/2 cups water
1 cup sugar
2 sticks cinnamon bark
4 whole cloves
4 cups unsweetened pineapple juice
1 cup orange juice
1/2 cup lemon juice

Combine water, sugar, and spices in saucepan and bring to a boil. Simmer for 5 minutes. Strain and cool. Add fruit juices and pour over ice into a tall pitcher or punch bowl.

Serves 4.

AUSTRALIA: PINEAPPLE MINT JULEP PUNCH

6 sprigs of fresh mint
3/4 cup powdered sugar
3/4 cup lemon juice
3 cups unsweetened pineapple juice, chilled
3 cups ginger ale, chilled

Wash mint. Discard stems and place leaves in a bowl. Bruise leaves with a spoon, then cover with powdered sugar. Add lemon juice and allow to stand about 15 minutes. Add pineapple juice and ginger ale.

Serves 6-8.

JAMAICA: FRUIT PUNCH

6 pints boiling water
5 teaspoons tea
5 teaspoons chopped mint
1-1/2 cups sugar
5 oranges, juiced
4 lemons, juiced
lemon slices
cracked ice

Pour the boiling water on the tea and mint. Let stand for a few minutes and then strain into a bowl.

Stir in the sugar until dissolved. Stir in the strained juice of the oranges and lemons and add some thinly peeled lemon rind.

Leave to stand 2 to 3 hours and then strain into a serving bowl over cracked ice. Garnish with slices of lemon cut very thinly.

JAMAICA: SPICED FRUIT PUNCH

2-1/2 cups orange juice
1 cup canned Jamaica pineapple
1/4 cup lemon juice
2 cups cold water
1/2 teaspoon nutmeg
1/4 teaspoon Jamaica allspice
1 tablespoon grated lemon rind
4 tablespoons Jamaica honey
6 whole cloves
6 cups ginger ale
crushed ice

Combine all ingredients except ginger ale and ice. Let chill for at least 3 hours. Strain. Add ginger ale and ice just before serving.
Makes about 3 quarts before adding ice.

Guam: Coconut Punch

6 young coconuts
1/2 pound sugar
3 tablespoons lemon juice
1 gallon water

Puncture the eyes of the coconuts, drain, and reserve the juice. Split coconuts and scrape out the meat. Combine coconut juice, coconut meat, sugar, lemon juice, and water. Add food coloring and ice as desired.

FRUIT

Punches

This chapter features traditional punches made from mixed fruit juices and served cold. Two of our favorites in this section are "Jewel Punch" and "Punch Served at the Nevada Executive Mansion" because of their unique presentation.

Jewel Punch

2 cans (6 ounces each) orange juice concentrate
2 cans (1 pint, 2 ounces each) grapefruit juice
1 46-ounce can tropical fruit punch
7-1/2 cups water
food coloring (red, yellow, blue, green)
6 cans (6 ounces each) lemonade concentrate
6 cans (6 ounces each) grapefruit concentrate
6 bottles (28 ounces each) club soda, chilled
12 bottles (28 ounces each) lemon-lime carbonated beverage

Make decorative ice cubes ahead:

Mix frozen orange juice with 2-1/2 cups water and a little red food coloring. Pour into 2 ice-cube trays and freeze.

Mix grapefruit juice with a little yellow food coloring. Freeze in 2 trays.

Mix tropical fruit punch with a little red food coloring and freeze in 2 trays.

Measure 2-1/2 cups water and mix with enough blue food coloring to make a medium shade of blue. Pour into an ice tray and freeze. Repeat using green food coloring.

At serving time, make punch:

Beat together lemonade and grapefruit concentrates (undiluted and still frozen). Pour half into punch bowl and add half of club soda, half of lemon-lime beverage, and half of the ice cubes. Keep remaining ingredients chilled and replenish punch as needed.

Serves 50.

Punch Served at the Nevada Executive Mansion

This recipe was shared with us by Grant Sawyer, former governor of Nevada, who enjoyed having this elegant punch served at the state's Executive Mansion. It features a rosebud ice ring that both garnishes and cools the punch.

1 large can frozen orange juice concentrate
2 cups very strong black tea (made with 1 cup of tea and 2 cups of boiling water)
4 cups sugar
1 quart fresh orange juice
1 large can unsweetened pineapple juice
2 quarts pink lemonade
cherry juice or red food coloring
24 tiny, perfect rosebuds with leaves
1 quart ginger ale, chilled
1 quart club soda, chilled

Day before: Make orange juice concentrate as directed on package. Mix with next four ingredients, then refrigerate.

To make frozen rosebud ring, begin by tinting pink lemonade with cherry juice or a few drops of red food coloring to intensify color. Then pour lemonade in ring mold to a depth of one inch. Freeze solid. Place rosebuds with leaves (face down) on frozen ring. Gently pour another inch of lemonade into ring mold and freeze. Then fill mold to within about an inch from top with lemonade and freeze solid.

Day of event: Pour half of fruit juice mixture into serving bowl. With clean hands, carefully remove frozen rosebud ring from mold and place in serving bowl. Add remaining fruit juice mixture. Add ginger ale and club soda.

Notes: If the punch ingredients are served ice cold, the ring will keep its shape for several hours. Also, maraschino cherries can be substituted for the rosebuds.

CHILDREN'S PARTY PUNCH

1 cup hot water
1/2 package strawberry- or cherry-flavored gelatin (Jell-O)
1/4 cup sugar
2-1/2 cups cold water
3/4 cup lemon juice
crushed ice
orange or lemon slices

Add hot water to gelatin and sugar. Stir until dissolved. Add cold water. Add lemon juice. Chill or pour over cracked ice. Serve with colored straws. Garnish with orange or lemon slices.

Serves 4-6.

FLAVORFUL FRUIT PUNCH FOR 50

1 cup water
2 cups sugar
1 cup strong hot tea
1 cup lemon juice
2 cups orange juice
2 cups pineapple juice
2 cups strawberry syrup (or jelly)
4 quarts cold water
1 cup maraschino cherries
1 quart soda water

Boil 1 cup water and sugar for 5 minutes, stirring until sugar is dissolved. Mix sugar syrup with tea and cool.

Add fruit juices and strawberry syrup. For strawberry syrup, use heavy fruit syrup from canned strawberries, or thin strawberry jelly with several tablespoons of warm water.

Let stand at least one hour in refrigerator. Just before serving, add remaining ingredients and pour over ice in punch bowl.

Serves 50.

Punch for 25

1 can frozen orange juice concentrate
1 can frozen lemon juice
1 bottle Hawaiian Punch, chilled
5 cups pineapple juice, chilled
1 quart ginger ale, chilled
7 cups water

Just before serving, combine all ingredients and pour over block of ice in punch bowl.

Fruit Punch Noel

4 cups apple cider
2 cups bottled cranberry juice
1 cup orange juice
1 twelve-ounce can apricot nectar
1 lemon
36 whole cloves
10 sugar cubes
1 teaspoon cinnamon

In a large saucepan, combine cider, cranberry juice, orange juice, and apricot nectar. Wash lemon and cut thinly into 12 slices. Insert 3 cloves in each slice. Add to fruit juices. Over very low heat, bring just to a simmer for 15 to 20 minutes. Pour into punch bowl.

In a small bowl, toss sugar lumps with cinnamon. Drop a sugar cube into each punch cup.

Makes 10 six-ounce servings.

PUNCH FOR 36

2 cups sugar
1 cup water
1 cup tea, hot or cold
2 cups syrup from cooked or canned fruit
1 cup lemon juice
2 cups orange juice
2 cups pineapple juice
ice water
1 quart carbonated water

Boil sugar and water for 5 minutes, stirring until sugar is dissolved. Add tea, fruit syrup, and juices. Let stand 30 minutes. Add ice water to make 1-1/2 gallons of liquid. Add carbonated water. Serve in punch bowl over block of ice.

Serves 36.

ROSY PARTY PUNCH

2 six-ounce cans frozen limeade
2 six-ounce cans pink lemonade
1 six-ounce can frozen orange juice
1 six-ounce can frozen grapefruit juice
10 cups water
2 quarts ginger ale or 7-Up
2 cups grenadine syrup

Makes about 1-1/2 gallons.

Kentucky Fruit Punch

3 sticks cinnamon
1 pint water
1 quart Hawaiian Punch
1 quart pineapple juice
1 pint orange juice
1 quart ginger ale
slices of oranges and pineapple

Boil cinnamon sticks in water for 10 minutes. Strain and cool. Add Hawaiian Punch and juices; chill well. Just before serving, pour over block of ice, add ginger ale, and garnish with orange and pineapple slices.

Quick Fruit Punch

frozen grape juice concentrate
frozen orange juice concentrate
frozen lemonade concentrate
1 quart sherbet
1 bottle ginger ale, chilled

Make juices from concentrate as directed on package and blend. Pour over sherbet in punch bowl and add ginger ale.

Blaine House Punch

4 cups fruit syrup (from canned fruit)
4 cups orange juice
4 cups pineapple juice
1 cup lemon juice
2 cups tea
2 quarts ginger ale, chilled
4-1/2 quarts ice water

Mix first five ingredients and chill well. Just before serving, add ginger ale and ice water.
Serves 50 or more.

Maryland Fruit Punch

3 cups water
2 cups sugar
2 six-ounce cans frozen lemonade concentrate, undiluted
8 six-ounce cans frozen orange juice concentrate, undiluted
16 cups cranberry juice
8 cups sparkling water

Boil water and sugar for 5 minutes, stirring until sugar is dissolved. Cool. Add juices and chill well. Just before serving, add cold sparkling water.
Serves 50.

Fruit Punch for 50

1 cup water
2 cups sugar
1 cup boiling water
2 teaspoons tea
2 cups fruit syrup (strawberry, raspberry, or mixed fruit)
1 cup lemon juice
2 cups orange juice
2 cups pineapple juice
6 cups ice water
1 quart soda water
1 cup maraschino cherries
block of ice

Boil water and sugar for five minutes, stirring until sugar is dissolved. In another saucepan, bring remaining 1 cup water to boil, remove from heat and add tea. Let stand 30 minutes.

Mix sugar syrup, tea, and fruit juices. Add enough ice water (about 6 cups) to make 1-1/2 gallons. Just before serving, add soda water and cherries. Serve in a punch bowl with a large block of ice.

Leftovers Punch

leftover juice from canned fruit
cranberry juice
1 can frozen lemonade concentrate
ginger ale or 7-Up
sugar (optional)

Save juices from canned fruit and mix with remaining ingredients to taste. Sweeten if desired with sugar.

South Carolina-Style Fruit Punch

2 small cans lemonade concentrate
2 large cans orange juice concentrate
2 large cans pineapple juice
1 large can orange juice
1 large can grapefruit juice
3 bottles ginger ale
sugar

Mix ingredients, adding sugar to taste. Serve over ice ring in punch bowl and garnish with fruit.

Montpelier Pink Punch

1 can frozen pink lemonade
1 quart cranberry juice
1 quart ginger ale
1 quart soda water

Prepare lemonade, adding enough water to make 1 quart. Add cranberry juice. Pour over ice in punch bowl. Add ginger ale and soda water.
Serves 32.

Virginia Fruit Punch

3 cans frozen orange juice concentrate
3 cans frozen lemonade concentrate
2 large cans pineapple juice
1 cup sugar (more if desired)
9 cups ice water (or less)
3 quarts ginger ale

Mix frozen concentrates, pineapple juice, sugar, and water, and chill. Pour over ice in punch bowl and add ginger ale just before serving.

Blended Fruit Punch

4 cans (13-1/2 ounce) apricot nectar
4 cans (13-1/2 ounce) pear nectar
4 cans (13-1/2 ounce) pineapple juice
2 cans (13-1/2 ounce) orange juice
2 cups ginger ale

Mix the first 4 ingredients. Chill. Pour over crushed ice and add ginger ale just before serving.
Serves 50.

Christmas Punch

4 quarts boiling water
4 tablespoons tea
3 cups sugar
4 (46-ounce) cans pineapple juice
5 dozen lemons (juiced)
4 (46-ounce) cans orange juice
4 quarts ginger ale, chilled
red and green maraschino cherries
orange slices

Pour boiling water over tea and let steep a few minutes. Strain. Sweeten to taste. When cold, add juices. Taste and add more sugar if necessary. Just before serving, pour over a large block of ice in punch bowl, add ginger ale, and garnish with cherries and orange slices. Pour the syrup from the cherries into the punch.
Serves 125.

Fruit Cooler

1-1/3 cups tea, chilled
3 tablespoons sugar
1/4 cup lemon juice, chilled
1 cup orange juice, chilled
1 twelve-ounce can apricot nectar, chilled
1 seven-ounce bottle ginger ale, chilled
ice cubes
6 fresh mint sprigs

Mix tea, sugar, and fruit juices in a 1-quart pitcher. Stir to mix well. Gradually add ginger ale. Serve over ice in tall glasses. Garnish with mint sprigs.
Serves 6.

Sherbet Punch

    2 quarts fruit juice
    1 gallon sherbet
    1 gallon ginger ale, chilled

Just before serving, whip fruit juice and sherbet with mixer, then add ginger ale. Good combinations of fruit juices and sherbet to try include grape juice with lemon sherbet, orange juice with lime sherbet, grape juice with grape sherbet, or cranberry juice with pineapple sherbet.

Serves 50.

Fruit Punch

    3 cups sugar
    1-1/2 cups water
    1 quart grape juice
    6 lemons, juiced
    6 oranges, juiced
    2 cups grated pineapple
    1 pint tea
    1 pint ginger ale
    2 quarts chilled water

Make sugar syrup by boiling sugar and water for 5 minutes, stirring until sugar is dissolved. Cool, then mix with juices, pineapple, and tea. Let stand in refrigerator at least 1 hour (or overnight).

Just before serving, add ginger ale and chilled water. Serve over crushed ice.

Serves 25.

Fruit Punch for a Crowd

1-1/2 cups sugar
2 cups hot tea
1 cup lemon juice, fresh-squeezed
5 cups orange juice, fresh-squeezed
2 quarts iced water
orange and lemon slices

Dissolve sugar in hot tea and let cool. Pour into gallon jar with fruit juices. Add iced water and keep cold until ready to use. Pour over ice in punch bowl. Garnish with fresh orange and lemon slices.
Serves 30.

Fruit Punch with Almond Flavoring

6 cups grapefruit juice
9-1/4 cups orange juice
3-1/2 cups canned crushed pineapple
1/2 cup lemon juice
1-3/4 cups lime juice
2 teaspoons almond flavoring
ice
orange and lemon slices
sprigs of mint

Combine first 6 ingredients. Chill well.
To serve, pour over ice and then garnish with orange and lemon slices and mint sprigs.
Serves 25.

Ginger Ale Fruit Punch for 50

4 six-ounce cans frozen lemonade concentrate
4 six-ounce cans frozen orange juice concentrate
16 cups water
2-1/2 cups pineapple juice
1 quart ginger ale

Mix all ingredients except ginger ale and chill well. Just before serving, add ginger ale.
Serves 50.

Ginger Ale Fruit Punch for 100

This recipe was shared with us by Mrs. George Wallace, whose husband served as the governor of Alabama for more than two decades.

1-1/2 quarts lemon juice
1-1/2 quarts orange juice
6 quarts water
4 pounds sugar
1 quart pineapple juice
2 quarts ginger ale

Mix first 5 ingredients and let stand several hours in ice. Add ginger ale. Serve in punch cups.
Serves 100.

Ginger Ale Punch

1-1/2 cups sugar
2 cups water
1/2 cup lemon juice
1 cup orange juice
1 cup grapefruit juice
4 cups ice water
1 pint ginger ale

Boil sugar and water 5 minutes, stirring until sugar is dissolved. Cool. Add remaining ingredients. Serve in glasses half filled with crushed ice.
Serves 15.

Hawaiian Fruit Punch for 50

3 six-ounce cans frozen pineapple juice
1 six-ounce can frozen orange juice concentrate
1 six-ounce can frozen lemonade concentrate
3 quarts cold water
1 cup strong tea
2 one-quart bottles ginger ale, chilled

Combine concentrates, water, and tea in a large punch bowl. Stir well. Add chilled ginger ale and ice and serve immediately.

For a Hawaiian touch, float a fresh flower or two in the punch and surround the bowl with a lei made by stringing green garden leaves on a thread.
Serves 50.

Golden Gate Julep

2 cups pineapple juice
1/4 cup lemon or lime juice
2/3 cup orange juice
2 tablespoons grenadine or maraschino cherry juice
fruit garnish

Combine first four ingredients. Chill. Serve over ice in tall glasses garnished with pineapple, maraschino cherry, and slice of orange.
Serves 4-6.

Harvard Punch

1 cup water
1-1/4 cups sugar
3 cups orange juice
1 cup lemon juice
1 cup pineapple juice
1 cup raspberry syrup
1-1/2 cups strong hot tea
1 quart soda water

Boil water and sugar for 5 minutes, stirring until sugar is dissolved. Cool. Mix with remaining ingredients except soda water. Just before serving, add soda water and pour over ice in a punch bowl.
Serves 30.

WISCONSIN PUNCH

2 large cans frozen orange juice concentrate
1 quart water
1 large can (46 ounce) pineapple juice
3 quarts sparkling water or ginger ale

Mix concentrate and water, chill well. Just before serving, add remaining ingredients and stir lightly. Pour over block of ice or ice cubes. Garnish with orange slices.

HOLLAND PUNCH

3 cups water
3 cups sugar
4 cups cranberry juice cocktail
3 cups lemon juice
2 cups orange juice
2 cups unsweetened pineapple juice
2 quarts ginger ale, chilled
mint sprigs

Boil water and sugar for 5 minutes, stirring until sugar is dissolved. Cool syrup. Add fruit juices and chill well. To serve, pour over ice in punch bowl and add ginger ale. Garnish with sprigs of mint.
Serves 50.

Mixed Fruit Punch (Four Fruits)

1-1/2 cups water
1-1/2 cups sugar
1 quart grape juice
6 lemons, juiced
6 oranges, juiced
1 pint tea
1 pint grated pineapple
2 quarts chilled water

Boil water and sugar for 10 minutes, stirring until sugar is dissolved. Cool and add fruit juices, tea, and pineapple; let stand 1 hour. Add 2 quarts chilled water, and serve over ice.

Serves 25.

Mixed Fruit Punch (Eight Fruits)

2 cups water
2 cups sugar
1 cup strawberries
1 cup raspberries
1 cup bananas
1 cup white grapes
1 cup pineapple juice
6 oranges, juiced
6 lemons, juiced
1 cup maraschino cherries
2 quarts soda water, chilled

Boil water and sugar 10 minutes, stirring until sugar is dissolved. Cool. In blender, puree strawberries, raspberries, bananas, and grapes. Mix sugar syrup, fruit puree, and fruit juices (including juice from cherries). Chill. Add soda water just before serving and garnish with cherries.

Serves 25.

Holly Punch

2 cups water
3 cups sugar
3 cups strong tea
6 cups orange juice
2 cups lemon juice
2 cups pineapple juice
2 cups raspberry syrup
2 quarts soda water, chilled

Boil water and sugar until sugar is thoroughly dissolved. Cool, then mix with tea, fruit juices, and raspberry syrup and allow to stand in the refrigerator for one hour. Just before serving, add soda water. To serve, pour over ice in punch bowl.
Serves 50.

Honolulu Punch

1 six-ounce can pineapple juice concentrate
3/4 cup cold water
28 ounces ginger ale, chilled
1 cup maraschino cherry juice or grenadine
whole strawberries

Combine concentrate and water, blending well. Add to ginger ale. Tint a delicate pink with maraschino cherry juice or grenadine, and float perfect whole strawberries just before serving.
Serves 10.

Papa's Punch

2-1/4 cups (20-ounce can) pineapple juice
2 cups orange juice
1 cup lemon juice
1 cup lime juice
1 cup sugar
1 quart ginger ale, chilled
1 quart carbonated water, chilled
1 box frozen whole strawberries

Combine fruit juices and sugar. Chill. Just before serving, add ginger ale, carbonated water, and frozen whole strawberries (to help keep drink chilled).
Serves 18-20.

Papaya Nectar

2 cups diced papaya
2 cups orange or pineapple juice
1/4 cup lime or lemon juice
1/4 cup passion fruit juice (optional)
1/4 cup honey

Puree papaya in blender and mix with other ingredients. Serve over ice in tall glasses.
Serves 4.

Party Punch for 20

1 cup sugar
2 cups tea, very strong
1 cup pineapple juice
1 cup maraschino cherry juice
1 large can grapefruit juice
1 cup lemon juice
1 cup orange juice
2 bottles ginger ale, chilled

Mix sugar with hot tea, stirring until sugar is dissolved. Add fruit juices. Just before serving, add ginger ale.

Serves about 20.

Party Punch for 50

1 can (46 ounce) pineapple-grapefruit juice
1 quart apple juice
3 cans (6 ounce) frozen orange juice concentrate
1 can (5-3/4 ounce) frozen lemonade concentrate
24 whole cloves
4 three-inch pieces cinnamon
1/2 teaspoon ginger
1/2 teaspoon ground allspice
1/2 teaspoon mace
6 whole cardamom
1/2 cup sugar
4 quarts ginger ale, chilled

Combine concentrates and fruit juices. Tie whole cloves in cheesecloth bag and add to juice. Add other spices and sugar. Mix well to dissolve sugar. Refrigerate several hours or overnight to chill and to allow flavors to blend. When ready to serve, remove spice bag. Pour into punch bowl over ice. Add ginger ale.

Serves 50.

Patio Punch

1 envelope cherry-flavored drink powder
1 envelope strawberry-flavored drink powder
2 cups sugar
2 quarts cold water
1 six-ounce can frozen orange juice concentrate
1 six-ounce can frozen lemonade concentrate
1 quart ice cubes
1 quart ginger ale, chilled

Combine drink powders and sugar. Add water and stir to dissolve. Add frozen concentrates. Pour over ice in punch bowl, then add ginger ale.
Serves 24.

Hollywood Punch

2 cups pineapple juice
1/2 cup lemon juice
2 cups orange juice
crushed ice
1 orange, quartered and thinly sliced
mint sprigs

Combine juices. Pour over crushed ice in tall glasses. Garnish with orange slices and mint.
Serves 6-8.

Punch for Receptions

2 cups water
4 cups sugar
2 cups strong black tea
10 lemons, juiced (about 2 cups)
10 oranges, juiced (about 2-1/2 cups)
12 ounces maraschino cherries with juice
3 gallons ice water
2 quarts ginger ale, chilled

Boil water and sugar together for 10 minutes, stirring until sugar is dissolved. Add tea and fruit juices (including juice from cherries). Chill several hours or overnight. Before serving, strain if desired and add cherries, water, and ginger ale.
Serves 75.

Fruit Medley Punch

1 can frozen lemonade concentrate
1 can frozen orange juice concentrate
1 can frozen grapefruit juice concentrate
1 can frozen tangerine juice concentrate
6 cups water
1 cup cold tea
2 quarts cold ginger ale

Combine juices, water, and tea; mix well. Add ginger ale. Pour over block of ice in punch bowl.
Serves 32.

Patriot Punch

1 can (6 ounce) frozen lemonade concentrate
1 can (6 ounce) orange juice concentrate
1 can (6 ounce) pineapple juice concentrate
3 bottles (28 ounces each) ginger ale, chilled
2 packages cherry-flavored drink mix
3 quarts ice water

Combine all ingredients and serve.
Serves 25.

Rainbow Punch

3 quarts pineapple juice
3 quarts raspberry juice
3 quarts lime juice
3 quarts loganberry juice
3 quarts grape juice
100 green cherries

Mix all ingredients, chill, and serve.
Serves 100.

Raindrop Punch

2 six-ounce cans lemonade concentrate
1 six-ounce can orange juice concentrate
1 six-ounce can concord grape juice concentrate
1 quart ginger ale, chilled

Prepare 1 can of lemonade concentrate with water as directed on package. Repeat with orange juice concentrate and grape juice concentrate. Fill one ice-cube tray with lemonade, one with orange juice, and one with grape juice and freeze. Pour leftover juices into a pitcher and chill. To serve, mix remaining can of lemonade concentrate with water as directed on package and add to pitcher. Pour ginger ale into pitcher and add frozen juice cubes. Serve from pitcher or in punch bowl.
Serves 12.

Red Fruit Punch

1/2 cup sugar
1 cup lemon juice
1 cup cherry juice
2 cups pineapple or pear juice
1 quart ginger ale, chilled

Mix sugar and juices. Cover and chill several hours or overnight until flavors are well blended. Just before serving, add ginger ale.
Serves 10.

Party Fruit Punch

3 cups sugar
1-1/2 cups water
1 quart grape juice
2 quarts chilled water
6 oranges, juiced
6 lemons, juiced
1 pint crushed pineapple or juice
1 pint tea
1 pint ginger ale

Boil sugar and water for 10 minutes, stirring until sugar is dissolved. Cool. Add fruit juices, tea, and water; let stand at least 1 hour or overnight. Add chilled ginger ale just before serving.
Serves 25.

Swimmer's Punch (Hot or Cold)

1 forty-six-ounce can pineapple-grapefruit juice drink
1 bottle cranberry juice cocktail
2 seven-ounce bottles lemon-lime soda
1 lemon cut into thin slices
16 whole cloves
4 tablespoons honey

Combine all ingredients in a large kettle and heat just below simmering point for 15 minutes. Strain and allow to cool. If making ahead, store in refrigerator. At party time, reheat or serve cold depending on the mood of the group.
Serves 6.

TROPICAL DELIGHT

1 cup water
1/2 cup sugar
4 whole cardamom seeds
1 three-inch stick cinnamon
1/8 teaspoon mace
1 forty-six-ounce can unsweetened grapefruit juice
1 twelve-ounce can apricot juice
1 twelve-ounce can papaya juice
1 twelve-ounce can guava nectar
1 twelve-ounce can pear nectar
28 ounces ginger ale, chilled

In saucepan, bring water, sugar, and spices to a boil and then reduce heat
and simmer 10 minutes. Cool and strain into combined juices. Add ginger ale
and serve over ice.
Serves 32.

TROPICAL PUNCH

1 cup lemon juice
1 large can (about 6 cups) passion fruit juice
1 large can (about 6 cups) pineapple-grapefruit juice
2 twenty-six-ounce bottles sparkling water

Combine fruit juices and chill. Just before serving, add sparkling water.
Pour over a block of ice in a punch bowl.
Serves 40.

Rose Water Punch

1/4 cup rose water
1 quart cold water
1 six-ounce can frozen lemonade concentrate
1 #2 can crushed pineapple, drained
2 cups crushed ice
fresh rose petals

Combine first four ingredients in a large bowl. Ladle into punch cups with crushed ice. Garnish each with a fresh rose petal.

Note: Rose water is water made fragrant with oil of roses. It is available in specialty grocery stores.

Serves 6.

Tutti-Frutti Punch with Banana

1 cup sugar
3 cups water
6 oranges, juiced
6 lemons, juiced
1 cup diced pineapple
1/2 cup maraschino cherries
2 sliced bananas
2 quarts soda water

Boil sugar and water until sugar dissolves. Cool. Add fruit juices and fruit. Pour over ice in punch bowl, adding soda water just before serving.

Serves 15.

Valentine Fruit Punch

1 small jar maraschino cherries
1 small can crushed pineapple
4 lemons, sliced
4 oranges, sliced
1 small bottle grape juice
1 bottle any fruit syrup
4 cups sugar
1 pint tea
red food coloring
4 cups water
crushed ice

Mix fruit, juice, syrup, and 2 cups of sugar and let stand an hour or longer. Strain. Add tea and enough food coloring to make a bright red.

In saucepan, boil remaining 2 cups sugar and water for 10 minutes. Cool. Add to punch, and add enough crushed ice to make it very cold.

Serves 10.

Royal Barley Water Punch

1/2 cup pearl barley
2-1/2 quarts boiling water
2 lemons
6 oranges
brown sugar

Add barley to boiling water in large saucepan, cover, and reduce heat. Simmer for 1 hour. Squeeze juice from lemons and oranges, reserving juice and rinds. Strain barley water into bowl. Add the rinds of 1 lemon and 3 oranges. Add sugar to taste. Allow to stand one hour. Strain, add orange and lemon juice, and chill well until serving.

Serves 25.

White Fruit Punch

3 cups sugar
2 quarts water
6 oranges, juiced
4 lemons, juiced
1 cup pineapple juice
1 cup peach juice
crushed ice

In saucepan, boil sugar and water 10 minutes. Cool. Add strained fruit juices and crushed ice.

Serves 18.

SLUSHY *Punches*

Perhaps because fruit punches are best when served icy cold, some of the best punches are slushy variations, which are especially refreshing during summertime. One of our favorites is "Orange Slush Punch for 10," which is delicious served as dessert after a family meal.

ORANGE SLUSH PUNCH FOR 10

1 pint orange juice, chilled
1 pint orange sherbet
1 pint vanilla ice cream
1 pint ginger ale, chilled

Beat orange juice, sherbet, and ice cream with mixer until just blended. Add ginger ale, stir lightly, and serve immediately.
Serves 10.

CREAMY PUNCH WITH SLICED CHERRIES

1 cup orange juice
1 cup unsweetened pineapple juice
1/4 cup lemon juice
1/4 cup maraschino cherry juice
2 tablespoons honey
1 pint vanilla ice cream
1 cup ginger ale, chilled
sliced maraschino cherries

Mix fruit juices and honey, stirring well. Chill for several hours or overnight. Just before serving, lightly whip ice cream and fruit juices with mixer. Add ginger ale, stir until just blended. Serve in tall glasses and top with cherry slices.
Makes 6 large servings.

Flossie's Sherbet Punch

2 six-ounce cans frozen lemonade
1 six-ounce can frozen orange juice concentrate
9 cups cold water
5 pints pineapple sherbet
1 quart vanilla ice cream

Just before serving, mix all together.
Serves about 50.

Frosty Fizz

2-1/2 cups water
2 cups sugar
5 cups unsweetened orange juice
2-1/2 cups unsweetened pineapple juice
2 cups lemon juice
1 quart ginger ale
1 seven-ounce bottle club soda
whole strawberries
lemon slices

Boil water and sugar for five minutes, then cool. Add fruit juices. Freeze in ice-cube trays until partially frozen (about 5 hours). To make ahead, freeze solid and then thaw for 3 hours before serving time.

Just before serving add ginger ale and club soda.

Punch is best when served in a partially frozen state. Garnish with whole strawberries and lemon slices.

Serves 35.

Slushy Party Punch

46 ounces (1 large can) grapefruit juice, frozen in can
46 ounces (1 large can) pineapple juice, frozen in can
46 ounces (1 large can) apple juice, frozen in can
12 ounces (1 can) frozen orange juice concentrate
6 cups cold water
5 cups sugar
2 quarts ginger ale

One hour before serving, remove frozen fruit juices and concentrate by cutting out both ends of each can and slipping contents into punch bowl. Add water and sugar, stir well, breaking apart concentrates. Add ginger ale. *Serves 50.*

Frosty Sherbet Punch

3 forty-six-ounce cans orange and grapefruit juice blend
3 twelve-ounce cans apricot nectar
3 quarts ginger ale
3 quarts pineapple sherbet

Chill juice and ginger ale thoroughly. Pour 1 can of each juice and 1 quart of ginger ale into the punch bowl. Add a quart of sherbet, and spoon the liquid over it until partly melted. When the supply runs low, repeat the process, adding another unit of each ingredient. This ensures that the punch stays cool and fresh throughout the event. *Serves about 80.*

Blender Lime Punch

1 six-ounce can frozen limeade concentrate
1 twelve-ounce package frozen mixed melon balls, thawed,
   or 1 ripe papaya, cut into small pieces
1 pear, peeled and cut into small pieces
3 cups water
2 cups cracked ice
few drops of green food coloring

Place half of each ingredient in the blender. Cover and blend until smooth for about 1 minute. Repeat with remaining ingredients. Mix and serve in tall glasses or in punch cups.
Makes 6 tall glasses or 12 punch cups.

Quick Frosty Cooler

1 pint lime or orange sherbet
1 quart ginger ale, chilled

Place a spoonful of sherbet into each punch cup, or spoon entire pint into a serving bowl. Pour ginger ale over sherbet. Serve immediately.
Serves 10.

FROSTY MINT CUP

30 fresh mint leaves, chopped
1/2 cup sugar
1 cup water
1 can limeade concentrate
1-1/2 quarts lime sherbet
16 sprigs of mint leaves
sugar

Boil chopped mint, sugar, and water for 10 minutes. Strain and chill liquid. Prepare limeade from concentrate, following instructions on can. Add 2 cups of limeade to chilled mixture and stir well. Just before serving, add sherbet, beating with mixer until frothy. Pour into sherbet cups. Garnish with mint sprigs.
Serves 16-18.

FROTHY FRUIT DRINK

1 egg white
1/3 cup honey
1/8 teaspoon salt
1 cup cold water
1-1/2 cups orange juice, chilled
1/3 cup lemon juice, chilled
4 cups crushed ice
mint sprigs

Beat egg white, honey, and salt with mixer until stiff enough to stand in peaks. Scrape into a 2-quart jar. Just before serving, add water and juices. Cover tightly and shake vigorously. Serve at once over crushed ice in tall glasses. Garnish with sprigs of mint.
Serves 6.

Frozen Fruit Punch

    6 cups water
    2 cups sugar
    1 small can orange juice concentrate, undiluted
    1 small can crushed pineapple, do not drain
    citric acid
    food coloring (optional)
    2 oranges, cut up
    2 lemons, cut up
    3 quarts ginger ale, chilled

Bring water and sugar to a boil until sugar is dissolved. Cool. Combine sugar syrup with orange juice and pineapple. Mix citric acid in 1/2 cup water, according to label directions. Add sparingly to fruit juice mixture, as it gives a tangy taste. Add food coloring, then add fruit pieces. Freeze punch. About 15 minutes before serving, place frozen punch in punch bowl and pour ginger ale over top.

Serves 25.

Lime Milk Punch

    1 quart milk
    1 quart lime sherbet, softened
    1 quart ginger ale
    food coloring

Mix milk and half of sherbet until well blended. Pour into punch bowl and add ginger ale. Float remaining sherbet in scoops on top.

For variation, orange or lemon sherbet can be substituted. If desired, add a few drops of food coloring after adding ginger ale for more intense color.

Serves 15.

Lime Punch for 50

2 quarts boiling water
2 tablespoons tea
3 dozen lemons
2 dozen oranges
sugar to taste
4 quarts ginger ale, chilled
2 gallons lime sherbet
orange or pineapple juice

Pour boiling water over tea and steep for 5 minutes. Strain and cool. Add juices from lemons and oranges, then sweeten to taste. Chill until ready to use. To serve pour into punch bowl, add ginger ale, and then place scoops of sherbet on top.

Replenish with cans of orange or pineapple juice if necessary.

Serves 50.

Lemon Julep

1 pint lemon sherbet
1 quart ginger ale, chilled
fresh mint
orange slices
maraschino cherries

Put lemon sherbet in glasses and fill with ginger ale. Garnish with sprigs of mint, orange slices, and cherries.

Note: For Orange Julep, substitute orange sherbet.

Serves 6.

Mrs. Guy's North Dakota Punch

4 quarts ginger ale, chilled
1/2 gallon lime sherbet
1 large can frozen limeade concentrate

Combine ginger ale with sherbet and frozen limeade concentrate in punch bowl. Serve immediately.

For variation, substitute orange sherbet and orange juice concentrate.

Refreshing Lime Sherbet Punch

1 quart milk sherbet, lime-flavored
2 quarts carbonated soda (or ginger ale)

Allow sherbet to melt slightly. Add carbonated soda at time of serving. For a variation, try other flavors of sherbet.

SPICED & MINTED

Punches

While a spiced punch served hot is traditionally served during cooler months, many variations are refreshing served cold in spring and summer.

English Wassail (Hot Cranberry)

1 teaspoon ground cloves
1 teaspoon allspice
1/2 teaspoon cinnamon
1/4 cup brown sugar
4 cups water
4 cups pineapple juice
4 cups orange juice
2 one-pound cans jellied cranberry sauce
few drops red food coloring
few bits butter

Combine spices, brown sugar, and water in saucepan. Boil for 3 minutes, reduce heat, and add pineapple and orange juices. Crush cranberry sauce through a sieve and add to mixture.

Bring to a boil. Simmer 5 minutes and remove from heat. Add red coloring and pour into heated punch bowl. Add butter. For trim, float clove-studded orange slices, cut in half.

Hawaiian Punch from Washington State

1 cup sugar
2 cups water
6 lemons (1 cup juice)
20 whole cloves
2 cups pineapple juice
2 cups orange juice
1 large bottle ginger ale, chilled

Dissolve sugar in water. Wash lemons, extract juice. Add several rinds and the cloves to the sugar-water mixture and bring to a boil.

Remove rinds and cloves. Add lemon, pineapple, and orange juices. Chill.

When ready to serve, pour into punch bowl and add ginger ale. For a festive look, float a frozen fruit ring in the bowl, an added Hawaiian touch.

CANTON GINGER PUNCH

1/2 pound Canton ginger
1 cup sugar
1 cup water
1/2 cup orange juice
1/2 cup lemon juice
1 quart soda water

Chop ginger, add sugar and 1 cup water. Boil 15 minutes. Add fruit juices, then strain. Add soda water. Pour over large piece of ice.
Serves 12.

SPICED GINGER PUNCH

2 cups sugar
2 cups water
15 cloves
1 three-inch stick of cinnamon
1/2 teaspoon ginger
3/4 cup lemon juice
2 cups orange juice
1 cup cider
few sprigs of mint

Boil sugar and water for 5 minutes, stirring until sugar is dissolved. Add spices, cover, and let cool. Add fruit juices. Strain. Pour over large block of ice and garnish with mint.
Serves 10.

Ginger Mint Punch

1/2 cup sugar
1 cup water
1/4 cup chopped mint leaves
1/2 cup lemon juice
2 cups orange juice
1 quart ginger ale
sprigs of fresh mint

Boil sugar and water for 5 minutes, stirring until sugar is dissolved. Add chopped mint leaves. Cool. Chill. To serve, strain and add fruit juices and ginger ale. Garnish with sprigs of fresh mint.
Serves 8.

Golden Mint Wedding Punch

42 mint sprigs
2 cups granulated sugar
2 quarts boiling water
2-1/3 cups lemon juice
2 quarts orange juice
1 #2 can pineapple juice
1 quart ginger ale
1 quart sparkling water
1 cup thinly slivered lemon rind

The day before the wedding: Wash mint. In 4-quart saucepan, heat sugar, water, and 30 mint sprigs, reserving remaining sprigs for garnish. Simmer, uncovered, for 10 minutes to make syrup. Strain mint syrup. Refrigerate overnight. Also refrigerate all other ingredients.

The wedding day: Just before serving, place mint syrup in punch bowl. Add fruit juices, ginger ale, and sparkling water. Top with 12 mint sprigs and lemon rind. Serve at once.
Serves 50.

Spiced Cranberry & Orange Punch

1/4 teaspoon ground cinnamon
1/4 teaspoon ground nutmeg
1/4 teaspoon ground allspice
4 pints cranberry juice cocktail
1 six-ounce can frozen orange juice, reconstituted
6 twelve-ounce bottles ginger ale

Combine all ingredients except ginger ale. Mix well and bring to a boil. Strain through cheesecloth if desired. Chill. Add chilled ginger ale just before serving.

Serves 40.

Hot Grape Punch

4 cups grape juice
1/4 cup sugar
1 teaspoon powdered cinnamon
1/4 teaspoon powdered nutmeg
1/8 teaspoon powdered cloves
1/8 teaspoon powdered ginger
5 cinnamon sticks

Combine all ingredients except cinnamon sticks in a kettle. Bring to a boil slowly. Serve hot with one cinnamon stick in each mug.

Serves 5.

Hot Spiced Grape Juice

1 teaspoon whole cloves
2-inch stick of cinnamon
1 quart grape juice
1-1/2 cups water
1/4 cup boiling water
1/2 teaspoon each of black and green tea
3/4 cup orange juice
3/4 cup lemon juice

Tie spices in a small cheesecloth bag. Place spices, grape juice, and water in saucepan and heat just to boiling. Remove from heat. Pour 1/4 cup boiling water over tea. Let steep five minutes. Add tea and remaining fruit juices to grape juice mixture. Let steep 4-6 hours, remove spice bag, reheat, and serve.
Serves 10.

Spiced Grape Punch

1 can limeade concentrate
1/2 teaspoon ground allspice
1/2 teaspoon ground cinnamon
1/2 teaspoon ground nutmeg
3 six-ounce cans frozen grape juice concentrate
6 twelve-ounce bottles ginger ale, chilled

Prepare limeade from concentrate according to label directions. Boil 1-1/2 cups limeade and spices in saucepan for 3 minutes. In pitcher or punch bowl, mix limeade with grape juice concentrate and ginger ale and serve.
Serves 25.

Punch on the Rocks

    5 quarts cocktail cranberry juice
    2 teaspoons grated lemon peel
    2 teaspoons grated orange peel
    20 whole cloves
    3 sticks cinnamon, broken
    1/4 cup lemon juice
    3 quarts apple juice
    orange slices
    lemon slices
    whole cloves

In saucepan, heat cranberry juice to almost boiling. Remove from heat and add lemon and orange peel and spices. Let cool for about an hour, then strain. Add other ingredients and chill. Garnish with orange and lemon slices studded with cloves.

Serves 20.

Red Clover Punch

    1 one-pound can sour cherries
    1/2 cup sugar
    8 whole cloves
    1 cup water
    1 cup apple juice
    red food coloring

Drain cherries, reserving juice. Mix cherries, sugar, cloves, and water. Boil 15 minutes, stirring frequently. Strain boiled mixture, pressing about half of the cherry pulp through sieve. Discard remaining pulp in sieve. Mix strained mixture with reserved cherry juice and apple juice. Add a drop of red food coloring. Chill.

Serves 6.

MULLED APRICOT NECTAR

1 forty-six-ounce can apricot nectar
1/2 cup orange juice
1/2 lemon, sliced
2 tablespoons honey
10 whole cloves
6 whole allspice
2 to 3 cinnamon sticks

Combine ingredients in a large saucepan. Cover. Simmer 10 minutes.
Remove from heat. Let stand 30 minutes. Reheat. Strain and serve.
Serves 8.

MULLED FRUIT PUNCH

2-1/2 cups unsweetened grapefruit juice
2-1/2 cups unsweetened pineapple juice
1/3 cup sugar
2 sticks cinnamon
1 teaspoon whole cloves

Combine all ingredients in saucepan. Place over low heat. Bring to a
boiling point. Simmer about 5 minutes. Strain. Serve hot in small cups.
Serves 8.

MULLED PINEAPPLE JUICE

1 forty-six-ounce can unsweetened pineapple juice
1 two-inch stick cinnamon
1/8 teaspoon nutmeg
1/8 teaspoon allspice
dash of ground cloves

Combine all ingredients in medium saucepan. Bring to boiling. Cover.
Reduce heat and simmer 30 minutes to blend flavors. Serve warm.
Serves 10.

Spiced Fruit Punch

2 cups boiling water
2 teaspoons tea
2 cups light corn syrup or 1-1/2 cups honey
dash of salt
1/4 teaspoon ground cloves
1 quart loganberry or any tart fruit juice
3/4 cup lemon juice
2 quarts ginger ale
sprig fresh mint
6 thin orange slices
6 whole cloves

Pour boiling water over tea. Cover and steep for 5 minutes. Strain. Combine with syrup or honey, salt, and cloves in 1-1/2 gallon enamel or glass container, stirring well. Cool. Add fruit juices, pour over ice in punch bowl, and then add ginger ale. Garnish with fresh mint and orange slices studded with cloves.

Makes about 4 quarts. Serves 24.

Mint Julep Punch

10 lemons, juiced
3 cups sugar
1 cup water
6 six-inch sprigs of bruised mint
6 pints ginger ale

In saucepan, mix juice, sugar, water, and mint sprigs. Bring to a boil. Cover and let stand about 30 minutes. Strain. Chill. Add ginger ale, then serve with crushed ice.

Serves 24.

Mint Punch

2 cups boiling water
1 quart mint leaves
2 cups white grape juice
1 quart strong lemonade
sugar
mint or fruit garnish

Pour boiling water over mint leaves and let stand until cold. Strain and add grape juice and lemonade. Mix all together. Sweeten to taste. Pour over ice. Garnish with sprig of mint or slice of lemon or orange.
Serves 12.

Mint Julep

1 bunch fresh mint
1-1/2 cups sugar
1/2 cup water
1 cup lemon juice
3 pints ginger ale, chilled

Add mint leaves, sugar, and water to lemon juice. Let stand 30 minutes. Pour over ice and add ginger ale.
Serves 10.

Spiced Pineapple Punch I

6 cups sugar
2 cups water
6 cinnamon sticks
1-1/2 teaspoons whole cloves
1 #10 can pineapple juice
1 #2 can pineapple juice

Boil sugar, water, cinnamon, and cloves. Strain and add to pineapple juice. Mix well and pour over crushed ice.
Serves 30.

Spiced Pineapple Punch II

3/4 cup sugar
1-2/3 cups water
12 whole cloves
1 forty-six-ounce can unsweetened pineapple juice
1-3/4 cups orange juice
3/4 cup lemon juice
1 bottle (28 ounces) ginger ale, chilled
12 cinnamon sticks

Simmer sugar, water, and spices for 15 minutes, covered. Strain and cool. Add fruit juices, then chill well. To serve, pour over ice and add ginger ale. Serve with cinnamon sticks as stirrers.
Serves 12.

Spiced Pine-Orange Punch

1 cup sugar
1-1/2 cups water
2 sticks cinnamon
8 whole cloves
4 cups unsweetened pineapple juice
1 cup orange juice
1/2 cup lemon juice

Combine sugar, water, and spices in saucepan. Place over low heat and boil for 3 to 5 minutes. Strain and cool. Add fruit juices. Pour over ice in pitcher or punch bowl.

Serves 8.

Spiced Rhubarb Cooler

2 pounds rhubarb
3 cups water
1-inch stick of cinnamon
4 whole cloves
1/8 teaspoon mace
1 cup sugar
1 cup water
2 tablespoons lemon juice
1/2 cup orange juice
1 pint ginger ale

Cut rhubarb in small pieces. Do not peel. Add water and spices. Simmer over low heat until tender and then strain. Meanwhile, boil sugar and water in saucepan for 7 minutes. Allow to cool. Mix rhubarb juice, sugar syrup, and fruit juices. Chill. To serve, pour over ice and add ginger ale.

Serves 6.

Yule Season Punch

2 cups water
1 cup sugar
4 cups cranberry juice
4 cinnamon sticks
12 whole cloves
1-1/2 cups lemon juice
2 cups orange juice
2 cups pineapple juice
1 quart ginger ale
lemon slices

Boil water and sugar until sugar dissolves, stirring frequently. Add cranberry juice and spices, cooking over low heat for 3 minutes. Remove from heat, strain, and let cool. Add fruit juices and chill well. To serve, add ginger ale. Float lemon slices on top.

Serves 15.

PUNCHES BY

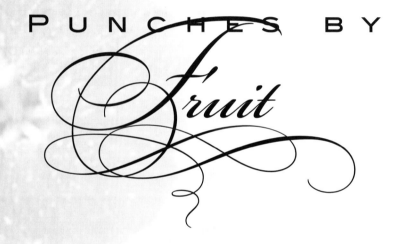

Fruit

When serving a punch that features a specific fruit, the punch bowl can be garnished with the featured fruit. See "Secrets to a Perfect Punch" for ideas on how to create garnishes. Also, for other punches featuring specific fruits, be sure to browse through our chapters on slushy punches and spiced and minted punches.

APPLE BLOSSOM COOLER

1 cup water
1/3 cup sugar
2 teaspoons mint leaves
1 three-inch piece cinnamon
1 quart apple juice
1/2 cup lemon juice

Bring water, sugar, mint leaves, and cinnamon to a boil. Reduce heat and simmer 10 minutes. Cool. Combine apple juice and lemon juice in a separate container. Strain syrup into juice mixture. Chill well before serving.
Serves 5.

APPLE BLOSSOM PUNCH

4 cups apple juice
1/2 cup lemon juice
2 cups apricot nectar
1/4 cup grenadine
block of ice
28 ounces ginger ale, chilled
1 pint lemon sherbet

Combine fruit juices and nectar with grenadine. Chill. Just before serving, pour over ice in punch bowl. Add ginger ale. Float scoops of lemon sherbet on surface.
Serves 15.

Jelly Punch

1/2 cup apple jelly (or other flavor)
1/4 cup sugar
1/2 cup lemon juice
1 cup water
1 quart ginger ale, chilled

Combine first 4 ingredients and beat until well blended. Add ginger ale. Other fruit jelly may be used instead of apple jelly.

Serves 10.

Pink Apple Punch

8 quarts chilled apple juice
16 bottles (7 ounces each) chilled lemon-lime carbonated
    beverage
3 one-pound jars maraschino cherries
red food coloring
ice cubes
4 to 8 lemons, sliced very thin

Combine apple juice, lemon-lime beverage, and syrup from maraschino cherries. Add a few drops of food coloring until desired shade of red is reached. Add ice cubes. Garnish with cherries and lemon slices.

Serves 50.

Apricot Punch

1-1/2 cups boiling water
1 tablespoon tea leaves
3 cups apricot nectar
1/2 cup lime juice
1-1/2 cups carbonated water

Pour boiling water over tea leaves. Steep 5 minutes. Strain and cool. Add fruit nectar and juice. Pour over ice in a pitcher. Add carbonated water.
Serves 12-15.

Autumn Gold Punch

3 cups apricot nectar
1-1/2 cups orange juice
3/4 cup lemon juice
1-1/2 quarts sweet cider
20 maraschino cherries

In a large pitcher, combine nectar, juices, and cider. Refrigerate until well chilled—at least 2 hours. Serve in punch cups garnished with cherries.
Serves 20.

Daffodil Punch

3 cups apricot nectar
2 cups pineapple juice
2 teaspoons vanilla

Mix all ingredients together and chill. Stir well before pouring into punch cups.
Serves 6.

Frosted Apricot Drink

1 cup cooked apricots and juice
3 cups milk
1/2 pint vanilla ice cream, softened

Press apricots through a sieve, discarding remains. Mix strained pulp with milk.

Place ice cream in a pitcher. Pour apricot milk mixture over ice cream. Stir until slightly mixed.

Serves 4-6.

Golden Punch

2 six-ounce cans frozen orange juice concentrate
2 six-ounce cans frozen lemonade concentrate
2 twelve-ounce cans apricot nectar
2 cans (1 pint 2 ounces each) pineapple juice

Prepare juices from frozen concentrate as directed on label. Combine with the apricot nectar and pineapple juice. Chill well before serving.

Serves 50.

Goldenrod Punch

2 #2-1/2 cans apricot halves
1 quart orange juice
1-1/2 cups lemon juice
1/2 cup lime juice
1 cup powdered sugar
4 quarts chilled sparkling water
ice

Press apricots (with juice from can) through sieve. Combine with other fruit juices and sugar. Strain if desired. To serve, add sparkling water. Pour over ice.
Serves 50.

Apricot Orange Blush

1 envelope (about 3 ounces) sweetened orange drink mix
1 twelve-ounce can apricot nectar, chilled
1 tablespoon lemon juice
6 orange slices

Prepare orange drink mix, following label directions. Stir in apricot nectar and lemon juice. Pour into 6 tall glasses. Garnish each with an orange slice.
Serves 6.

BLACKBERRY SHRUB

2 gallons blackberries
5 ounces tartaric acid
sugar
water

Crush berries slightly. Mix acid in water until dissolved. Pour over berries and let stand for 48 hours. Strain. Do not press—allow to drip. To each pint of juice add 3/4 cup of sugar. Mix well and let stand for a week or two, lightly covered.

Bottle and cork. Store in a cool place. When using, add one part blackberry mixture to 4 parts chilled water. Use crushed ice and more sugar if necessary.
Serves 50.

LOGAN PUNCH

1/2 cup boiling water
2 teaspoons orange pekoe tea
1/2 cup sugar
few grains of salt
1 cup loganberry juice
2 lemons, juiced
1 pint ginger ale
small bunch fresh mint

Let tea stand in boiling water 2 minutes. Strain. Add sugar and salt. Cool. Add fruit juices and ginger ale. Pour over cracked ice, and garnish with mint sprigs.
Serves 4-6.

Loganberry Punch

1 quart lemon juice
1 quart loganberry juice
2/3 quart orange juice
loganberry syrup to taste
carbonated water

Mix juices and syrup together and add a small amount of carbonated water.
Serves 24.

Loganberry, Jr.

7 thirteen-and-one-half-ounce cans loganberry juice
3 thirteen-and-one-half-ounce cans grapefruit juice
2 thirteen-and-one-half-ounce cans orange juice
2 thirteen-and-one-half-ounce cans apricot nectar

Mix all ingredients. Chill and serve.
Serves 50.

Raspberry Punch

2 cups orange juice
1-1/2 cups lemonade
2 packages frozen red raspberries
3/4 cup sugar
dash of grated lemon rind
1 pint ice water
1 quart ginger ale, chilled

Mix orange juice and lemonade. Thaw raspberries. Crush one package, mix with sugar, and blend with fruit juices and lemon rind. Chill. Strain if desired. Just before serving, add ice water, ginger ale, and remaining raspberries.

Serves 15.

Pink Lady

3 cups sugar
6 cups water
6 cups raspberry syrup, chilled
1-1/2 cups lemon juice, chilled
6 quarts pineapple juice, chilled
6 quarts sparkling water, chilled

Boil sugar and water 5 minutes, stirring until sugar dissolves. Cool. Combine with raspberry syrup and fruit juices. Add sparkling water just before serving.

Serves 50.

Raspberry Shrub

1 ten-ounce package frozen raspberries
3 cups water
1/4 cup fresh lime juice
grated rind of 1 lime
1 lemon, juiced
1/4 cup sugar
1 cup canned tangerine juice

Boil raspberries with 2 cups of water for 5 minutes. Strain boiled mixture, pressing berries through sieve into the strained liquid. Add remaining ingredients, mix well, and chill.
Serves 8.

Raspberry Sparkle

1/2 small box raspberry-flavored gelatin (Jell-O)
2 cups hot water
2 cups cold water
3 tablespoons lime juice
ice cubes
lime wedges

Dissolve gelatin in hot water in a pitcher. As soon as gelatin is dissolved, add cold water and lime juice. Serve over ice cubes in tall glasses. Garnish each with lime wedges threaded onto a fancy toothpick.
Serves 4.

Raspberry-Syrup Punch

8 ten-ounce boxes frozen raspberries
4 cups sliced fresh pineapple
3/4 cup lemon juice
2 cups white corn syrup
ice water (enough to make a total of 2 gallons)
3 quarts ginger ale, chilled
whole strawberries

Thaw raspberries and crush them with pineapple, lemon juice, and syrup. Let stand for several hours. Strain and force some of the pulp through the strainer with the juice. Just before serving time, pour the mixture into the punch bowl over a block of ice. Add ice water and ginger ale. Float fresh strawberries on top.

Serves 48.

Tom Sawyer Punch

1 #300 can blueberries
1 cup blueberry juice (drained from the berries)
1 cup water
1/2 cup grape juice
1 cup grapefruit juice

Drain blueberries, reserving juice. Boil berries in water for 10 minutes. Strain and press through sieve. Mix fruit juices (including 1 cup of reserved blueberry juice) with strained blueberry mixture. Chill and serve.

Serves 8.

FRUIT-BERRY PUNCH

1 cup strong tea
1/2 cup lemon juice
1 cup orange juice
1 cup pineapple juice
1/2 cup blackberry juice
1/2 cup raspberry juice
sugar
1 pint carbonated water
mint leaves
lemon slices

Combine the tea and fruit juices. Sweeten with sugar to taste. Chill thoroughly in refrigerator. Add the carbonated water to the fruit juices. Mix and pour over and around a large block of ice or ice cubes in punch bowl. Garnish with mint and lemon slices.

Serves 15.

Citrus Cooler

1-1/2 cups grape juice
2 cups fresh lemon juice
3 cups fresh orange juice
1-1/2 cups sugar
2 quarts water
orange and lemon slices

Mix juices and sugar. Cover and chill 4 to 8 hours to allow flavors to blend. Pour over block of ice in punch bowl. Garnish with orange and lemon slices.
Serves 30.

Dreamland Punch

2 dozen eggs
6 cups sugar
2 teaspoons salt
3 cups orange marmalade, chilled
5 quarts orange juice, chilled
3 cups lemon juice, chilled
4 quarts ginger ale, chilled

Beat eggs with sugar and salt thoroughly. Add marmalade and fruit juices one at a time, beating well after each addition. Just before serving, add ginger ale.
Serves 50.

Lemon and Lime Mist

1/2 cup lemon juice, chilled
1/4 cup lime juice, chilled
2/3 cup granulated sugar
1-1/4 cups club soda, chilled
1/2 cup crushed ice

Combine all ingredients in blender. Blend at high speed, covered, about half a minute. Pour into chilled glasses. Garnish with flowers.
Makes 6 three-ounce servings.

Lime Blossom Cooler

2 teaspoons grated lime rind
1 cup fresh lime juice
3/4 cup sugar
green food coloring
4 twelve-ounce bottles lemon-lime flavored carbonated beverage
ice cubes
1 large lime, sliced thin

Combine lime rind, juice, and sugar. Add a few drops of green food coloring and stir until sugar dissolves. Stir in carbonated beverage. Pour over ice in 6 tall glasses. Float 1 or 2 lime slices on top of each.
Serves 6.

Party-Tangerine Punch

1 package tangerine drink mix
1/2 cup sugar
2 quarts cold water
1 to 2 cans (6 ounce) frozen lemonade concentrate

Put soft-drink mix into a tall pitcher. Add sugar, water, and one can of lemonade concentrate. Stir to combine. Taste. Add more concentrate as desired. Chill. Serve over ice.

Serves 6.

Pink Party Punch

1 six-ounce can frozen lemonade concentrate
3/4 cup grapefruit juice
1/2 cup orange juice
1 pint white grape juice, chilled
1 pint carbonated water
1 quart ginger ale, chilled
1/4 cup grenadine

Combine concentrate and fruit juices. Chill. Just before serving, add carbonated water, ginger ale, and grenadine. Blend well. Serve immediately.

Serves 18.

Pink Polynesian Punch

2 #2 cans pineapple-grapefruit juice drink
6 cups orange juice
1 cup lemon juice
1 cup grenadine syrup
crushed ice

Blend fruit juices and flavorings in a pitcher. To make the punch foamy, fill blender or shaker jar 1/3 full of crushed ice. Add about 1/4 of fruit juice mixture and agitate until foamy. Repeat to make enough to serve, preparing more as needed.
Serves 12.

Quince Blossom Punch

2 cups grapefruit juice
2 cups orange juice
1 cup maraschino cherry juice

Mix fruit juices, chill, and serve.
Serves 10.

Nonalcoholic Planter's Punch

1 cup lime juice
1 cup orange juice
1 cup granulated sugar
1 eight-ounce jar maraschino cherries
1/2 teaspoon rum flavoring
1 tray ice cubes
orange and lime slices

In a blender or drink shaker, combine lime juice, orange juice, sugar, 1-1/2 teaspoons maraschino cherry juice, and rum flavoring. Blend at low speed or shake for 1 minute.

Pour over ice cubes in pitcher. Stir well. Let stand 20 minutes. Strain into chilled glasses. Garnish each with orange and lime slice and cherry speared on a fancy toothpick.

Serves 4.

Nonalcoholic Planter's Punch for One

1 tablespoon sugar
3 tablespoons water
1/8 teaspoon rum flavoring
1 lime, juiced
crushed ice
1 slice orange
1 slice pineapple
1 cherry

In a tall glass, dissolve sugar in water. Add rum flavoring and lime juice. Fill with crushed ice. Stir until outside is coated like a mint julep. Garnish with orange and lime slices and a cherry speared on a fancy toothpick or straw.

Serves 1.

HOLIDAY CRANBERRY PUNCH

2 pints cranberry juice cocktail
1 six-ounce can pineapple juice
1 quart apple juice
1 six-ounce can frozen lemonade concentrate
1 six-ounce can frozen grapefruit juice concentrate
2 bottles carbonated water
12 orange slices

Chill liquids. Just before serving, mix fruit juices with frozen concentrate, then pour over block of ice in punch bowl. Add carbonated water. Stir lightly. Garnish with orange slices.
Serves 24.

HOLIDAY PUNCH

1 quart orange sherbet
1 quart cranberry juice
1 pint fresh orange juice
2 seven-ounce bottles ginger ale

Chill all ingredients well. Just before serving, place orange sherbet in punch bowl. Pour other ingredients over sherbet, adding ginger ale last.

CRANBERRY ROYAL PUNCH

2 pints cranberry juice cocktail, chilled
2 cups pineapple juice, chilled
1-1/2 cups sugar
2 quarts ginger ale, chilled
ice

Combine juices with sugar. Just before serving, add ginger ale and ice.
Serves 20.

CRANBERRY PINEAPPLE PUNCH

1 forty-six-ounce can pineapple-grapefruit juice drink
1 cup canned whole cranberry sauce
1/2 cup crushed pineapple
1 quart ginger ale

Chill all ingredients. At serving time, mix together in punch bowl. Add
enough ice cubes to keep punch cold.
Serves 16.

HOT CRANBERRY JUICE

6 cups cranberries
4 cups water
1 cup light corn syrup
1 cup white sugar

In saucepan, simmer all ingredients until berries are soft. Strain through
double cheesecloth. Reheat when ready to serve.
Serves 6.

CRANBERRY-TEA PUNCH

1 quart strong tea
1 quart cranberry juice cocktail
1 cup strained lemon juice
2 cups strained orange juice
1 quart water
1/2 cup sugar
1 quart ginger ale, chilled

Mix tea, fruit juices, water, and sugar. Chill for several hours. Just before serving, add ginger ale. Pour over large piece of ice in a punch bowl.
Serves 25.

CRANBERRY JUICE PUNCH

1-1/2 cups sugar
1/2 cup water
4 cups cranberry juice
1 cup pineapple juice
1 cup orange juice
2 cups lemon juice
1 cup ginger ale

Boil sugar and water for 5 minutes, stirring until sugar is dissolved. Add fruit juices. Just before serving, add ginger ale.
Serves 12.

Sparkling Cranberry Punch

1 large can jellied cranberry sauce
2-1/4 cups water
1/2 cup sugar
1/2 cup lemon juice
1 teaspoon almond extract
1-1/2 cups ginger ale
mint
clove-studded lemon slices

Crush cranberry sauce in can with fork, then empty into saucepan. Beat with rotary beater. Add water and beat until sauce is melted. Add sugar, then cool. Stir in lemon juice, almond extract, and 1 cup of ginger ale. Just before serving, dilute with remaining 1/2 cup ginger ale. Serve well iced in frosted glasses. Garnish with mint and clove-studded lemon circles.

Serves 12.

Hot Cranberry Punch

4 pints cranberry juice cocktail
4 six-ounce cans frozen lemonade, undiluted
1/2 teaspoon salt
1 teaspoon ground allspice
4 cups water
15 three-inch pieces cinnamon

Combine all ingredients except cinnamon. Simmer 10 to 15 minutes. Do not boil. Serve hot in mugs, using cinnamon sticks as stirrers.

Serves 15.

Pink Cranberry Punch

1/2 cup sugar
3 pints orange juice
3 pints cranberry juice
1 quart ginger ale

Mix sugar with orange juice and combine with cranberry juice. Add ginger ale just before serving.
Serves 30-32.

Cranberry Julep

4 cups sugar
4 cups water
3 cups cranberry juice
1/4 cup lemon juice
1 quart ginger ale
sprigs of mint
1 orange, quartered and cut into thin slices

Boil sugar and water together for 5 minutes, stirring until sugar is dissolved. Cool. Combine fruit juices and ginger ale. Add sugar syrup to taste. Pour over large piece of ice in a pitcher or bowl garnished with mint and orange slices.
Serves 15.

Hot, Buttered, Bright-red Cranberry Punch

1/2 to 3/4 cup brown sugar, firmly packed
1/4 teaspoon salt
1/4 teaspoon nutmeg
1/2 teaspoon cinnamon
1/2 teaspoon allspice
3/4 teaspoon ground cloves
4 cups water
2 one-pound cans jellied cranberry sauce
1 quart canned pineapple juice
butter
whole cinnamon sticks

Bring sugar, spices, and 1 cup of the water to a boil, simmer and stir until sugar is dissolved. Remove from heat.

In a large saucepan, crush cranberry sauce with a fork and add remaining 3 cups of water. Beat until smooth. Add pineapple juice and the spiced syrup. Simmer about 5 minutes. Serve hot, topped with butter. Use cinnamon sticks for stirrers. Serve this bright-red punch piping hot.

Serves 20.

Hot Spiced Cranberry Punch

1 quart cider or grape juice
1 quart cranberry juice
6 cloves
1 three-inch stick of cinnamon
4 whole allspice
1/2 cup brown sugar

Mix all ingredients in a large pot. Heat slowly until the sugar dissolves. Do not boil. Serve hot.

Serves 12.

CRANBERRY FRUIT PUNCH

2 cups sugar
1 cup water
1 cup strong tea
1 bottle cranberry juice cocktail
2 cups orange juice
1 cup lemon juice
1 quart ice water
2 bottles ginger ale, chilled

Boil sugar and water for five minutes, stirring until sugar is dissolved. Cool, then add tea and fruit juices. Just before serving, add ice water and ginger ale.
Serves 35-40.

CRANBERRY SPARKLE

1/4 teaspoon ground cinnamon
1/4 teaspoon ground nutmeg
1/4 teaspoon ground allspice
4 pints cranberry juice cocktail
1 quart orange juice
6 king-size bottles ginger ale, chilled

Combine all ingredients except ginger ale. Mix well. Strain through cheesecloth, if desired. Chill. Add ginger ale just before serving.
Serves 42.

CRANBERRY PUNCH I

2 cups sugar
1 cup water
2 cups lemon juice
2 cups crushed pineapple or juice
1-1/2 cups orange juice
3 cups cranberry juice
1 cup strong tea
1 quart water
1 quart ginger ale, chilled
fruit garnish

In saucepan, bring sugar and water to a boil, then simmer and stir until sugar is dissolved. Cool. Mix with fruit juices, tea, and water. Just before serving, add ginger ale. Garnish with orange and lemon slices and minted green cherries.

Serves 35-40.

CRANBERRY PUNCH II

2 cups water
1 cup sugar
1 quart cranberry juice
1 six-ounce can frozen pineapple juice
1 quart ginger ale, chilled
1 quart club soda, chilled

Boil water and sugar for five minutes, stirring until sugar dissolves. Cool. Mix with fruit juices and chill well. Just before serving, add ginger ale and club soda.

Serves 20-24.

Rosy Cranberry Punch

2 pints cranberry juice cocktail
2-1/2 cups water
1/2 cup lemon juice
1/3 cup sugar
1/4 teaspoon nutmeg
1/4 teaspoon cinnamon
1/4 teaspoon salt
1/8 teaspoon cloves
cinnamon sticks

Combine ingredients in saucepan. Simmer 10 minutes. Serve hot in mugs.
Use cinnamon sticks as stirrers.
Serves 10.

Ruby Cup

2 one-pound cans strained cranberry juice
1 quart apple juice
2 oranges, juiced
1 lemon, juiced

Mix all ingredients, blending well. Bring to a boil. Remove from heat.
Serve hot.
Serves 10.

CRANBERRY-ORANGE PUNCH

1 gallon cranberry juice
2 quarts orange juice
1/2 cup lime juice or lemon juice
1 to 1-1/2 cups sugar
2 quarts sherbet

Combine fruit juices and sugar, stirring until well blended. Chill well.
Just before serving, pour in a punch bowl. Add 2 quarts of a fruit sherbet such as orange, strawberry, or raspberry for richness.
Serves 36.

PINK CLOUD COOLER

2 cups cranberry juice cocktail, chilled
2 drops almond extract
1/2 cup skim milk
2 tablespoons lemon juice

Combine ingredients in shaker or blender. Shake or mix until smooth and creamy. Serve over crushed ice. Garnish with cherry and pineapple chunks on a toothpick.
Serves 4-6.

Grape Punch for 35

2 cups sugar
2 cups water
1 quart grape juice
1 large can frozen lemonade concentrate
1 large can frozen orange juice concentrate
2 cups strong tea, chilled
1-1/2 quarts ginger ale, chilled
1 large can crushed pineapple, chilled

Boil sugar and water for five minutes, stirring until sugar dissolves. Cool. Add grape juice, frozen juice concentrates, and tea. Before serving, add ginger ale and crushed pineapple.

Serves 35.

Grape Punch for 6

mint
1/2 cup sugar
1 lemon, juiced
1/2 cup pineapple, crushed
2 cups pineapple juice
2 cups grape juice
cherries

Crush mint, mix with sugar and lemon juice, stirring well. Add pineapple and fruit juices. Cool. Serve over ice and garnish with cherries.

Serves 6.

Grape Juice Punch for 18

    1 quart grape juice
    4 lemons, juiced
    4 oranges, juiced
    1-1/2 cups sugar
    2 quarts soda water

Mix fruit juices and sugar, stirring well. Pour over a block of ice in punch bowl, then add soda water.
Serves 18.

Grape Juice Punch for 40

    2 quarts grape juice
    1 cup lemon juice
    block of ice
    1 gallon soda water, chilled
    1 quart ginger ale, chilled
    sugar

Mix fruit juices and chill well. Just before serving, pour fruit juices over block of ice in punch bowl, then add the soda water and ginger ale. If desired, add sugar to taste.
Serves 40.

Spiced Grape Juice Punch

4 lemons
1 handful borage (herb)
1 cup sugar
1 stick cinnamon
1 quart grape juice, chilled
1 quart ice water
mint

Squeeze juice from lemons into bowl and mix with borage, sugar, and cinnamon stick. Let stand one hour. Add grape juice and ice water. Pour over a large block of ice in punch bowl and garnish with mint.
Serves 12.

Grape-Fruit Punch

1/2 cup orange juice
1/2 cup lemon juice
1 pint grape juice
1 pint ginger ale, chilled

Mix fruit juices and chill well. Add ginger ale just before serving.
Serves 8.

Grape Cooler

1/2 cup sugar
2 cups water
1 cup grape juice
1 cup orange juice
1/2 cup lemon juice
1 quart ginger ale

Boil sugar and water for five minutes, stirring until sugar is dissolved. Cool. Add fruit juices. Pour over ice in pitcher, and then add ginger ale.
Serves 6-8.

Lemon-Orange-Grape Juice Punch

3 lemons, juiced
2 oranges, juiced
1 pint grape juice
2 cups water
1 cup sugar
1 pint ginger ale
cherries or mint sprigs

Combine juices, water, and sugar. Stand in refrigerator several hours. When ready to serve, add ginger ale and mix thoroughly. Pour over ice and garnish with cherries or mint sprigs.
Serves 25.

Montreaux Grape Cup

3 whole cardamoms
6 tablespoons sugar
1-1/2 cups water
stick of cinnamon, broken to make 1 teaspoon
1 cup grape juice

Break open cardamom shells and remove tiny seeds. Discard shells. Boil sugar, water, cardamom seeds, and cinnamon for 10 minutes. Strain. Add grape juice. Chill and serve.
Serves 6.

Royal Grape Punch

2 cups boiling water
5 teaspoons tea
1/2 cup sugar
12 to 15 ice cubes
1 pint grape juice
2 oranges, juiced
2 lemons, juiced
1 twelve-ounce bottle ginger ale, chilled
2 oranges, thinly sliced
2 lemons, thinly sliced

Pour boiling water over tea and let stand 10 minutes. Strain, add sugar, and stir until dissolved. Pour over ice in a pitcher or punch bowl. Add fruit juices. Just before serving, add ginger ale and garnish with paper-thin slices of lemon and orange.
Serves 14.

PEACH PUNCH

    1/2 pound sugar
    1 quart water
    1 gallon peach concentrate
    1/2 pint pineapple juice
    1 teaspoon salt
    1 quart ginger ale

Boil sugar and water together for five minutes, cool. Mix all ingredients except ginger ale and chill well (overnight if possible). Just before serving, pour punch concentrate in punch bowl, then add ginger ale.

Note: If you cannot find peach concentrate, make it at home by peeling and pitting fresh, ripe peaches and then processing in a blender or mashing them thoroughly by hand (a potato masher works well).

FRESH PEACH BLEND

    3 medium-sized ripe peaches
    2 tablespoons sugar
    1/4 cup cold water
    1-1/2 cups chipped ice

Wash and quarter peaches, removing pits. Do not peel. Place in an electric blender. Add sugar, water, and ice. Blend at high speed. Serve immediately in chilled glasses.

Serves 4.

GOLD PUNCH

1/2 pound dried peaches
3/4 cup sugar
1 cup orange juice
1/4 cup lemon juice
1 cup pineapple juice
2 quarts ice water
1 orange, cut in paper-thin slices and quartered
sprigs of fresh mint

Cook peaches until soft. Add sugar and cook a few more minutes until sugar is dissolved. Press fruit mixture through a sieve, then mix with fruit juices. Strain if desired for a smoother consistency. Mix with ice water, and serve garnished with orange slices and mint.

Serves 15.

FROTHY PINEAPPLE-GINGER ALE PUNCH

6 forty-six-ounce cans pineapple juice
6 quarts ginger ale
6 six-ounce cans frozen lemonade
orange or lemon sherbet

Combine first three ingredients and refrigerate for 2 days. Just before serving, fill tall glasses 3/4 full with punch mixture and then spoon sherbet into glasses.

Serves 50.

MEXICAN PINK PUNCH

2 large pineapples
8 lemons, juiced
1/2 teaspoon cloves
3 cups granulated sugar
4 cups water
grenadine

Peel and core pineapple. Cut pineapple into small pieces and puree in blender. Mix with lemon juice, cloves, and sugar, blending well. Add water. Cover and let stand about 8 hours at room temperature. Strain. Before serving, add grenadine to color pink and additional sugar to taste.

Makes 16 small glasses.

Pineapple Mint Punch

1 cup mint jelly
3 cups boiling water
1 cup orange juice
1 cup pineapple juice
1/2 cup lemon juice
12 ounces ginger ale, chilled

Dissolve mint jelly in boiling water. Add fruit juices, chill. Just before serving, add ginger ale. Pour over ice.
Serves 12.

Pineapple Mint Punch with Milk

12 mint leaves
3 cups cold milk
3/4 cup cream
1-1/2 teaspoons lemon juice
2 cups cold pineapple juice
1/4 cup sugar
dash of salt

Crush mint leaves in bowl before mixing. Remove leaves and discard. Combine remaining ingredients in bowl and beat until foamy. Pour into tall glasses. Garnish with mint and serve immediately.
Serves 6.

Pineapple Mint Julep

6 sprigs fresh mint
3/4 cup sugar
3/4 cup lemon juice
3 cups unsweetened pineapple juice
3 cups ginger ale

Wash mint leaves; bruise with spoon. Cover with sugar. Add lemon juice. Let stand about 15 minutes. Add pineapple juice. Pour over ice in pitcher or tall glasses. Add ginger ale. Garnish with sprigs of mint.
Serves 8.

Pineapple-Raspberryade

ginger ale
1 cup water
1 cup canned crushed pineapple
1 cup canned raspberry juice
1 lemon, juiced

Pour ginger ale into ice-cube trays and freeze. Mix remaining ingredients and keep in refrigerator until ready to serve. To serve, fill glasses with ginger ale cubes and add punch.
Serves 8.

Pineapple Foam

2 cups pineapple juice
1/4 cup lemon juice
2 egg whites
1 quart ginger ale, chilled

Place all ingredients except ginger ale into a cocktail shaker or canning jar with lid. Shake well. Serve over crushed ice in tall glasses, filling glass halfway with juice mixture and then filling with ginger ale.

Serves 10.

Round the World Punch

3 cups sugar
3 cups hot water
1 forty-six-ounce can pineapple juice
3/4 cup lemon juice
3 pints sparkling water
fresh or frozen strawberries

Dissolve sugar in hot water. Cool. Add juices and chill. To serve, add sparkling water. Decorate punch bowl with small strawberries.

Serves 30.

Rhubarb Punch

1 cup tea
2 lemons, juiced (6 tablespoons)
1/2 cup honey
8 sprigs of mint
1 stick of cinnamon
1/8 teaspoon salt
2 cups rhubarb juice
1 quart cold water
orange slices
mint sprigs

Mix tea, lemon juice, and honey, stirring well. Add mint, cinnamon stick, and salt. Make rhubarb juice by boiling rhubarb in small amount of water. Add rhubarb juice to tea mixture and chill well. Before serving, remove cinnamon stick and add water. Serve over ice, garnishing each glass with an orange slice and a sprig of mint.

Serves 12.

Rhubarb Toast

5 cups rhubarb, cut into small pieces
1 quart water
2 cups sugar
1 cup pineapple or orange juice
1/4 cup lemon juice
ginger ale, chilled

Cook rhubarb with water until very tender. Strain through a fine strainer or cloth. Add sugar and bring to a boil, stirring constantly. Cool. Add fruit juices. Pour over large block of ice and add an equal amount of ginger ale or other carbonated beverage.

Serves 18.

Rhubarb Punch with Ginger Ale

4 cups rhubarb cut into small pieces
4 cups water
1 cup white sugar
1/2 cup brown sugar
1/2 can undiluted frozen orange juice concentrate
2/3 cup lemon juice
1/4 teaspoon salt
1 quart ginger ale, chilled

Combine rhubarb and water in a saucepan and cook over low heat until rhubarb is very tender. Strain rhubarb and return to saucepan. Add white and brown sugar to rhubarb juice. Heat, stirring constantly until sugar is dissolved. Add fruit juices and salt. Remove from heat. Place in electric blender and beat for 1 minute, or use rotary beater for 3 minutes. Cool and chill. When ready to serve, add ginger ale and serve over ice.

Serves 24.

Rhubarb Orange-Lemon Punch

1-1/2 pounds rhubarb
1 quart water
1-1/2 cups sugar
1/3 cup orange juice
4 tablespoons lemon juice
few grains of salt
1 quart soda water or ginger ale, chilled

Cut rhubarb into small pieces and boil in water until very tender. Strain, squeezing well, through a double thickness of cheesecloth. Return juice to saucepan and add sugar, stirring well until sugar is dissolved. Heat to boiling point. Add fruit juices and salt. Chill. To serve, add soda water or ginger ale and pour into large pitcher or punch bowl over ice.

Serves 12.

Punch with Floating Strawberries

1 pint strawberries
1 cup mint leaves
3 quarts unsweetened pineapple juice
8 lemons, juiced
8 oranges, juiced
3 limes, juiced
2 cups sugar
4 quarts dry ginger ale, chilled
2 quarts plain soda water, chilled

Place strawberries on tray and freeze for several hours (at least 3 hours). Bruise mint leaves in large bowl or pitcher. Add fruit juices and sugar, chill thoroughly. Just before serving, pour juice mixture over ice in punch bowl. Add ginger ale and soda water. Float frozen strawberries on top.
Serves 35.

Strawberry Sparkle

2 tablespoons strawberry-flavored drink mix
1/4 cup cold water
2 teaspoons lemon juice
1/4 cup chilled sparkling water
1 whole strawberry

Mix strawberry drink mix with water and lemon juice. To serve, add sparkling water and pour over crushed ice. Garnish with fresh strawberry.
Serves 1.

STRAWBERRY FRUIT PUNCH FOR 14

4 cups water
4 cups sugar
5 oranges, juiced
5 lemons, juiced
1 cup pineapple juice
1 cup sliced pineapple
2 quarts hulled strawberries
2 quarts carbonated water
4 cups crushed ice

Boil water and sugar for five minutes, stirring until sugar is dissolved. Cool. Mix sugar syrup, fruit juices, and fruit and chill well.

Just before serving, add carbonated water and crushed ice. Water may be added if too strong.

Serves 14.

STRAWBERRY FRUIT PUNCH FOR 50

3 cups boiling water
4 tablespoons tea leaves
3 cups sugar
1-1/2 quarts cold water
3 cups orange juice
1-1/2 cups lemon juice
3 cups strawberries, sliced and sweetened
1-1/2 quarts ginger ale, chilled

Pour boiling water over tea leaves. Steep for 5 minutes. Strain and pour hot tea over sugar. Stir until dissolved. Cool and add cold water, fruit juices, and strawberries. Pour over ice in punch bowl. Just before serving, add ginger ale.

Serves 50.

STRAWBERRY BLOOM PUNCH

1 ten-ounce box frozen strawberries
1 pint water
1/4 cup sugar
1 six-ounce can frozen lemonade concentrate

Boil strawberries, water, and sugar 5 minutes. Strain, pressing berries through sieve. Prepare lemonade as directed on label. Add 2-1/2 cups of lemonade to strained juice. Chill well before serving.
Serves 16.

STRAWBERRY FESTIVAL PUNCH

2 cups sugar
1 cup water
1-1/2 cups strong hot tea
1 six-ounce can frozen lemon juice
1 six-ounce can frozen orange juice
1 six-ounce can frozen grapefruit juice
2 quarts ice water
2-1/2 cups (#2 can) pineapple chunks
4 quarts soda water, cold
2 ten-ounce packages frozen strawberries

Boil sugar and water for 5 minutes, stirring until sugar is dissolved. Add tea, fruit juices, ice water, and pineapple chunks (including juice from can). Let stand several hours. To serve, add soda water and pour over block of ice in punch bowl. Break apart frozen strawberries and float on top of punch.
Serves 80.

Cider

A favorite on frosty nights during the autumn season, cider is a spiced drink that is usually served piping hot but can be served chilled for gatherings in warmer weather.

Our favorite cider garnish is candied apples, featured in the "Floating Apple Wassail" recipe. This floating garnish could be used to enhance any cider recipe.

Floating Apple Wassail

3/4 cup red cinnamon drops
1/2 cup granulated sugar
1 cup white corn syrup
1-1/2 cups water
10 crab apples or lady apples
4 lemons, sliced
12 whole cloves
1 gallon apple cider
22 whole cinnamon sticks
water

Make apple garnish day before or early in the day:

In a saucepan, combine cinnamon, sugar, corn syrup, and water. Cook, stirring often, until mixture boils. Continue to boil, without stirring, until a small amount of sugar syrup dropped into very cold water separates into threads that are hard but not brittle. Remove syrup from heat. Quickly coat apples in syrup one at a time, removing each from pan with slotted spoon. Place on greased cookie sheet to cool. Store in a cool, dry place.

Make wassail about an hour before serving:

Stud lemon slices with cloves. In a kettle, combine cider, lemon slices, and cinnamon sticks. Bring to a boil. Cover and simmer about 45 minutes.

With slotted spoon, remove lemon slices and cinnamon. Pour steaming punch into serving bowl and add apples, which will bob on top. Ladle wassail into punch cups with cinnamon sticks as swizzlers. Serve the apples with punch if desired.

Serves 20.

Cider Punch

1/3 cup sugar
1/3 cup water
2/3 cup orange juice
1/3 cup lemon juice
1-1/3 cup cider
1 cup ginger ale or carbonated water, chilled

Boil sugar and water for 5 minutes, stirring until sugar is dissolved. Cool, then add fruit juices and cider. Chill well.

Before serving, add ginger ale or carbonated water and pour over ice and serve.

Serves 6.

Grape Cider Punch

4 sticks cinnamon
24 whole cloves or 1 teaspoon allspice
5 cups sweet cider or apple juice
4 cups grape juice
1/2 cup lemon juice
1 teaspoon grated lemon rind
1 teaspoon grated orange rind
2 quarts ginger ale, chilled

Combine spices and 2 cups of cider in a saucepan. Place over low heat, bring to a boil, and simmer about 5 minutes. Remove from heat. Let stand 30 minutes and strain. Add remaining cider, grape juice, lemon juice, lemon rind, and orange rind. Pour into jars or pitchers. Chill. When ready to serve, pour over ice in punch bowl and add ginger ale. Garnish with orange slices.

Serves 35-40.

Mulled Cider

1 quart cider
2 whole cloves
2 whole allspice
1 three-inch stick cinnamon
3/8 cup brown sugar

Boil cider and spices for 5 minutes. Just before serving, add sugar and boil another 5 minutes.
Serves 6.

Spiced Cider

1 quart cider
1/4 cup sugar
dash of salt
12 whole cloves
2 four-inch cinnamon sticks
8 whole allspice

Combine all ingredients in a 2-quart saucepan. Bring to a boil, stirring until sugar is dissolved. Cool. Cover and refrigerate several hours to chill and to allow flavors to blend.

Just before serving, warm in microwave oven until hot or over low heat on stove top, slowly increasing heat. Strain to remove spices. Serve hot in mugs or punch cups.
Serves 8.

Hot Spiced Cider

1 orange
1 lemon
1 quart cider
1/2 teaspoon whole allspice
1/4 teaspoon whole cloves
2 sticks of cinnamon broken in pieces
sugar

Thinly slice orange and lemon and add to cider and spices in a saucepan. Heat slowly until it reaches a boil. Remove from heat, strain, and serve hot, adding sugar to taste. Can be made a day ahead and reheated. Recipe can be quadrupled to make a gallon.
Serves 8.

Thanksgiving Cider

3 oranges, juiced
3 lemons, juiced
3 cups canned or bottled apricot juice
1-1/2 quarts sweet cider
crushed ice
1 dozen green maraschino cherries
1 dozen red maraschino cherries

Combine juices and cider. Chill well. To serve, fill tall glasses with crushed ice and garnish with cherries. Fill glasses with cider.
Serves 12.

HOT CINNAMON CIDER PUNCH

3 oranges
3 lemons
1 cinnamon stick
1 tablespoon allspice
1-1/2 quarts water
1-1/2 cups sugar
1 gallon sweet cider

Squeeze juice from the oranges and lemons. Place rinds, spices, and water in a saucepan. Cover and simmer 2-1/2 hours. Strain. Add sugar, fruit juices, and cider. Heat almost to the boiling point. Do not boil. Serve hot.
Serves 30.

HOT PINEAPPLE CIDER

1 cup fresh mint leaves
1 quart cider
2 cups unsweetened pineapple juice
4 cups ginger ale (room temperature)

Crush mint leaves and combine with cider and pineapple juice. Bring to a boil. Strain and bring to a boil again. Remove from heat, add ginger ale, and serve immediately.
Serves 12.

October Cider Punch

1/2 cup sugar
1/2 cup boiling water
3 quarts sweet cider
1 pint pineapple juice
1/2 cup lemon juice
1 cup orange juice
1 quart bottle soda water
fresh fruit for garnish

Add sugar to boiling water, stir well. Add cider and fruit juices. Chill well. Just before serving add soda water. Garnish with sliced fresh fruit.
Serves 30.

Hot Wassail

2 large oranges
2 lemons
1-1/2 quarts water
2 sticks cinnamon
2 tablespoons whole cloves
1 cup sugar
1 gallon cider

Squeeze juice from oranges and lemons, reserving both juice and rinds. In saucepan, mix rinds with water, spices, and sugar. Simmer in covered saucepan about 1 hour. Strain and add cider and reserved fruit juices. Reheat, but do not boil. Serve hot.
Serves 36-40.

Autumn Harvest Punch

1 quart fresh or bottled cider
3/4 cup lemon juice
sugar
ice
1 quart carbonated water

Mix cider and lemon juice. Sweeten to taste with sugar (or sugar syrup), then strain into punch bowl over a large block of ice. Just before serving add carbonated water.

Serves 8.

Autumn Harvest Brew

2 cups granulated sugar
4 quarts water
2 six-ounce cans frozen lemonade concentrate
1 tablespoon honey
2 quarts apple cider
1 quart cranberry juice
1 pint orange juice
1 pint strong black tea

Boil sugar and water for 5 minutes, stirring well until sugar is dissolved. Add remaining ingredients. Chill thoroughly before serving.

Serves 40.

Hot Buttered Rum Punch

2 quarts hard cider
1/2 cup brown or maple sugar
dash of salt
1/2 cup butter
2 teaspoons rum flavoring
powdered cinnamon

Heat cider until beads form on the surface, but do not boil. Remove from heat. Add sugar, salt, and butter. Stir until thoroughly blended. Add rum flavoring.

To serve, pour into punch cup and sprinkle with cinnamon.

Serves 8.

COCOA & MILK-BASED Drinks

Nearly any cocoa recipe is enhanced when served topped with a heaping spoonful of freshly whipped cream and chocolate shavings. To grate chocolate for the shavings, chill the chocolate first and use a cheese grater. For longer curls, use room-temperature chocolate and shave it with a vegetable peeler. Consider heating cocoa in the microwave oven, stirring frequently, rather than on the stove top where scorching can occur.

Rich Hot Chocolate for 50

1 pound unsweetened baking chocolate
4 cups hot water
2 gallons milk
2 quarts evaporated milk, undiluted
4 cups sugar

In microwave oven or double boiler, melt chocolate in the hot water, stirring frequently until thoroughly dissolved and smooth. In separate saucepan, combine milk and evaporated milk and scald, heating until tiny bubbles form around edges. Add sugar to milk, stir until dissolved. Blend both mixtures together, stirring until smooth. If desired, add more sugar to taste. Can be served hot or cold.

Serves 50.

Spiced Cocoa

1/2 cup cocoa
1/2 cup sugar
1/2 cup water
3 two-inch cinnamon sticks
12 whole cloves
5 cups milk
whipped cream
nutmeg

Combine cocoa and sugar in saucepan. Add water, stirring until dissolved. Add spices. Place over low heat and bring to a boil. Boil about 5 minutes, stirring constantly. Add milk. Heat to boiling point and strain. Serve hot in mugs or chill thoroughly and serve in tall glasses. Top with whipped cream and sprinkled nutmeg.

Serves 6-8.

Bachelor's Chocolate

2 squares unsweetened chocolate (2 ounces)
1 cup water
pinch of salt
3 to 4 tablespoons sugar
3 cups milk
whipped cream

Over low heat, melt chocolate in water, stirring until chocolate melts. Add salt and sugar. Boil 4 minutes while stirring constantly.

Slowly stir in milk and heat until scalded (when tiny bubbles form around the edges). Do not boil.

Just before serving, beat until smooth. Top with whipped cream. Serve hot. *Serves 6.*

Italian Cioccolata

4 cups milk
4 tablespoons cocoa
2 tablespoons sugar
1/2 teaspoon salt, dissolved in a little water

Scald the milk in top of a double boiler or in microwave, heating until tiny bubbles form at edges. (Do not boil.) Add cocoa, sugar, and salt. Cook for 15 minutes just below boiling point. Beat well and serve immediately. *Serves 4.*

Party Cocoa

1-1/2 cups cocoa
1-1/2 cups sugar
1/4 teaspoon salt
1 cup hot water
2 teaspoons vanilla
1 pint whipping cream
1 gallon hot milk

Mix cocoa, sugar, salt, and hot water. Cook until thickened. Add vanilla. Cool.

In separate container, whip cream until stiff. By spoonfuls, add condensed chocolate syrup to whipped cream and beat. Continue adding chocolate syrup until cream begins to lose its stiffness.

Just before serving, scald milk (heating until tiny bubbles form at edges). Place one to two spoonfuls of whipped cream mixture in each cup , then fill cups with of hot milk and stir.

Note: Chocolate syrup also can be used as hot fudge sauce over ice cream (omit whipped cream).

Serves 16.

Italian Chiaro D'Uovo Al Latte (Egg Flip)

2 cups milk
1-1/2 teaspoons honey
2 egg whites

Scald milk, heating until tiny bubbles form at edges. Cook for 10 minutes just below boiling point. Remove from heat and add honey, stirring until dissolved thoroughly. In separate bowl, beat egg whites until stiff, then fold into milk mixture. Serve hot or cold.

Serves 2.

Russian Chocolate

1 cup sugar
1/2 cup water
2 cups hot chocolate
2 cups hot coffee
4 teaspoons whipping cream or coffee cream
crushed ice
whipped cream
cherries

Make sugar syrup by boiling sugar and water for 5 minutes, stirring until sugar is dissolved. Remove from heat.

Combine hot chocolate and hot coffee, then add 1/2 cup of sugar syrup and 4 teaspoons of cream. Cool and place in refrigerator to chill. Place glasses in refrigerator to frost. When ready to serve, pour chilled beverage into frosted glasses filled with crushed ice.

Garnish with whipped cream and cherries.

Serves 6.

BUTTERMILK PUNCH

1 quart buttermilk
1 teaspoon cinnamon
1/2 teaspoon nutmeg
grated lemon rind
2 tablespoons lemon juice
4 to 5 tablespoons sugar
1 cup heavy cream, whipped
ice cubes

Beat the buttermilk until frothy. Add all the seasonings to taste. Blend in the whipped cream and serve mixture in a large pitcher with 4 or 5 ice cubes. *Serves 6-8.*

MOLASSES PUNCH

6 cups milk
1/4 cup molasses
1/8 teaspoon salt
1/2 teaspoon ginger

Blend milk and molasses. Add salt and ginger, serve. *Serves 6.*

SOUTHLAND MINT SMOOTHIE

2 cups skim milk
2 tablespoons molasses
few drops of peppermint flavoring
crushed ice
mint sprigs

Stir molasses into milk. Add peppermint flavoring. Pour into tall glasses filled with crushed ice. Garnish with mint sprigs.

Serves 2.

Coffee

Good coffee requires a clean, freshly scalded pot, accurately measured coffee, and fresh water. Serve the coffee immediately after brewing. For best taste, follow these tips:

Airtight storage. *Coffee loses its flavor when exposed to air, so keep it tightly covered. Buy drip grind for automatic coffeemakers with glass pitchers and regular grind for percolators and for boiling coffee in a pot.*

Frequent cleaning. *To avoid coffeepot stains, which can ruin the taste of fresh coffee, wash coffeemakers with soap and water after each use. Occasionally boil water and 1 cup of baking soda or salt in the pot to remove stain buildup.*

Brewing secrets. *Bring fresh cold water to a rolling boil before adding coffee to the pot. For best results, brew coffee at the full capacity of the coffeemaker, then place a piece of waxed paper into the spout of the coffee pot to prevent the flavor and steam of the coffee from escaping.*

Serving cold. *The secret of good iced coffee is a strong coffee base. When the strong coffee is poured over ice and diluted, a true coffee flavor is achieved. Serve in tall glasses and offer sugar and cream as with hot coffee.*

Coffee Punch à la Mode

1-1/2 pints ice cream (vanilla or part vanilla and part chocolate)
4 cups hot coffee
grated nutmeg

Pour coffee over ice cream, then beat lightly until ice cream is partially melted and floating in small pieces. Pour into punch glasses and sprinkle with nutmeg.
Serves 8.

Coffee Punch

1 quart vanilla ice cream
1 cup whipped cream
1/2 cup powdered sugar
2 quarts ice-cold strong coffee
1 teaspoon vanilla flavoring

Combine the ingredients in a punch bowl. Beat lightly with mixer until just blended. Serve at once.
Serves 20.

Java Cream Punch

4 cups strong coffee freshly brewed
1 cup heavy cream or evaporated milk
1/2 teaspoon vanilla
1 quart vanilla ice cream

Chill coffee. Whip cream or evaporated milk, add vanilla. With mixer, beat coffee and ice cream. Fold whipped cream into coffee, and serve immediately.
Serves 15.

Frosted Coffee Hawaiian

2 cups strong coffee, chilled
1 pint coffee ice cream, softened
1 cup pineapple juice, chilled
1/2 cup orange juice, chilled
1/4 teaspoon nutmeg

Combine ingredients and beat with mixer until mixture is smooth and foamy. Serve immediately in tall glasses.
Serves 4-5.

TURKISH COFFEE

1/2 cup water
1 tablespoon sesame seeds
1 tablespoon honey
3 tablespoons instant coffee

Combine water, sesame seeds, and honey. Bring to a rolling boil. Reduce heat. Cover and simmer for 5 minutes. Remove from heat. Add coffee. Strain into cups.
Serves 2.

QUICK ICED COFFEE

1 teaspoon instant coffee
1 teaspoon sugar
1/4 teaspoon evaporated milk, chilled
1/4 cup chilled sparkling water

Mix coffee, sugar, and evaporated milk, stirring until smooth. Add sparkling water. Pour over crushed ice. Sprinkle with cinnamon.
Serves 1.

COFFEE FOR THE CROWD

1 egg
1-1/4 pound coffee
1 cup cold water
9 quarts cold water

Mix entire egg (shell and all) with coffee. Add 1 cup cold water. Tie coffee in a cheesecloth bag large enough to allow room for coffee to swell. Pour 9 quarts chilled water into large pot. Immerse coffee bag into water. Bring to a boil.

Remove pot from heat. Leave bag of coffee in water 3 to 4 minutes, then discard coffee grounds and serve.
Makes 48 cups.

Coffee Float

1/2 cup sugar
2 cups water
dash of salt
1-1/2 tablespoons instant coffee
1 pint vanilla ice cream
carbonated water

Combine sugar, water, and salt in saucepan and simmer 5 minutes. Add coffee to hot liquid, stir. Cool. Pour into 4 tall glasses until 2/3 full. Add a tablespoon of ice cream to each glass. Fill almost to top with carbonated water. Slip another scoop of ice cream into each glass and serve.

Serves 4.

Dutch Coffee

6 cinnamon sticks
6 tablespoons heavy cream
6 cups freshly brewed coffee
6 pats of butter
sugar

Place a cinnamon stick and 1 tablespoon of cream in each cup. Fill cups with freshly brewed coffee and float a pat of butter on top. Serve with sugar.

Serves 6.

SOUTHERN COFFEE PUNCH

2 quarts strong coffee, chilled
1 pint cold milk
2 teaspoons vanilla
1/2 cup sugar
1 quart vanilla ice cream
1/2 pint heavy cream, whipped
nutmeg

Combine coffee, milk, vanilla, and sugar in large bowl. Stir until sugar is dissolved. Keep chilled. At serving time, place ice cream in punch bowl, pour coffee mixture over ice cream, then top with whipped cream. Sprinkle with nutmeg.
Serves 15-18.

COFFEE BANANA MILK PUNCH

2 medium, fully ripe bananas
3 cups milk
1/4 cup sugar
2 teaspoons instant coffee
1 teaspoon pure vanilla extract
whipped cream

Slice bananas, then mash and mix with 1/2 cup milk. Mix sugar with instant coffee and add to mixture. Stir in remaining milk and vanilla extract. Beat with electric mixer. Garnish with whipped cream.
Serves 6.

South American Coffee Punch

    8 cinnamon sticks
    1 gallon hot strong coffee
    1/4 cup sugar
    4 teaspoons vanilla
    2 quarts coffee ice cream
    1 quart whipping cream, whipped

Add cinnamon sticks to coffee. After coffee cools, remove cinnamon sticks and mix in sugar, vanilla, ice cream, and half the whipped cream. Float more whipped cream on top.

Serve from a punch bowl into tall iced glasses partially filled with finely chipped ice.

Serves 30.

South American Fizz

    1/2 teaspoon instant coffee
    1/2 teaspoon sweetened chocolate-flavored drink mix
    1/2 teaspoon sugar
    1/2 cup water
    crushed ice
    1 ten-ounce bottle lemon-flavored carbonated beverage
    4 orange slices
    4 maraschino cherries

Combine instant coffee, chocolate-flavored drink mix, sugar, and water in a cup. Stir until dissolved. To serve, fill 2 glasses with crushed ice. Fill glasses half with coffee mixture and half with lemon-flavored beverage. Garnish with orange slices and maraschino cherries threaded on fancy toothpicks.

Serves 2.

Mocha Punch

2 quarts freshly made coffee
2 quarts chocolate ice cream
4 tablespoons rum flavoring
1 quart heavy cream, whipped
grated sweet chocolate for garnish

Chill coffee and punch bowl. Mix coffee and half of ice cream in punch bowl, lightly beating with mixer until just blended.

Add remaining ice cream and rum flavoring, stirring until partly melted. Stir in the rum flavoring and 2-1/2 cups of whipped cream. Serve in tall glasses, topped with a spoonful of remaining whipped cream and sprinkled with grated chocolate.

Serves 25.

The Milkman's Punch

1-1/2 pints chocolate ice cream
1 quart coffee, double strength, chilled
3/4 cup heavy cream
1/4 teaspoon almond flavoring
nutmeg

Place half of chocolate ice cream in punch bowl. Add chilled coffee. Stir until ice cream is partially melted. Whip cream. Add flavoring. Pile lightly on coffee mixture. Sprinkle with nutmeg. Place remaining ice cream in center or arrange in small dips in each glass.

Serves 12.

Witches' Brew for Halloween

4 cups strong, hot coffee
2 medium, unpeeled oranges, sliced thin
sugar to taste
1/2 cup heavy cream
2 tablespoons sugar
1 tablespoon grated orange peel
shaved unsweetened chocolate

Pour coffee over sliced oranges. Let stand 30 minutes. Strain coffee and then reheat to just below boiling point. Sweeten if desired. Whip cream, blending in 2 tablespoons sugar. To serve, pour coffee into mugs, float whipped cream on top, and garnish with orange peel and chocolate shavings.
Serves 4.

Eggnog

A favorite during winter holidays, eggnog is traditionally flavored with vanilla flavoring and nutmeg. We have rounded up several refreshing variations that use flavorings such as orange, chocolate, coffee, cinnamon, and even pineapple. As in all recipes calling for raw eggs, eggnog should be made immediately before serving, and any unused portions should be discarded.

Orange Eggnog

6 eggs
1/4 cup granulated sugar
1/4 teaspoon cinnamon
1/4 teaspoon ginger
1/4 teaspoon ground cloves
2 quarts refrigerated orange juice
1/2 cup lemon juice
1 quart vanilla ice cream, softened
1 quart refrigerated ginger ale
nutmeg

Beat eggs until light colored. Add sugar and spices. Stir in orange and lemon juices.

Just before serving, use a small melon scoop to scoop ice cream into punch bowl. Pour juice mixture and ginger ale over ice cream. Sprinkle with nutmeg.

Serves 20-25.

Orange Eggnog for One

1 egg
1 tablespoon lemon juice
1/2 cup orange juice
1 tablespoon corn syrup

Beat egg well. Add other ingredients and mix thoroughly. Chill. Serve ice cold.

Serves 1.

Eggnog in a Hurry

2 quarts commercially prepared eggnog
4 egg whites
nutmeg

Pour chilled eggnog into punch bowl. For a frothy topping, beat egg whites. Spoon onto top of punch. Sprinkle with nutmeg. Recipe can be cut in half to serve a small gathering of six.
Serves 12.

Coffee Nog

2 eggs
1 cup strong coffee (warm)
1/2 cup sugar
dash salt
1 teaspoon vanilla flavoring
2 cups cream

Separate eggs. Beat egg yolks well, then add coffee, sugar, and salt, blending well after each addition. Cook in double boiler over hot water (or in microwave oven) until thick. Remove and cool. Add flavoring. Whip egg whites and cream until thick but not stiff. Fold into coffee mixture.
Serves 4.

Coffee Eggnog for One

1 egg
1-1/2 teaspoons sugar
1/2 cup strong cold coffee
1/2 cup cream or milk

Separate egg. Beat egg yolk and sugar. In separate bowl, beat egg white until stiff. Mix egg yolk and egg white, then stir in coffee and cream or milk.
Serves 1.

Eggnog for Four

2 eggs
1 to 2 tablespoons sugar
2 cups milk
1/2 teaspoon vanilla

Separate eggs. Beat egg whites until stiff but not dry. In another bowl, beat egg yolks well, then add sugar and milk, beating well after each addition. Add vanilla. Fold in egg whites.
Serves 4.

Hot Pineapple Eggnog

16 eggs
2 cups sugar
1 #10 can pineapple juice
1 quart cream
1/4 cup grated orange rind

Separate eggs. Add 1 cup sugar to egg yolks and beat well. Divide egg whites in half. Add half of egg whites to egg yolk mixture, beat thoroughly.

Bring pineapple juice to a boil. Add cream, reheat, and then slowly pour into egg yolk mixture, stirring constantly. Beat remaining egg whites, add remaining sugar, and beat well. Fold egg white mixture into hot mixture. Sprinkle with grated orange rind.
Serves 50.

Chocolate Eggnog

6 eggs
2 quarts chocolate milk
1/2 cup honey
1-1/2 cups heavy cream, whipped

Beat eggs well. Alternately add chocolate milk and honey a little at a time, beating well after each addition. Fold in all but a few tablespoons of the whipped cream. Pour into pitchers and top with reserved cream.
Serves 18.

Mocha Eggnog

2 eggs, separated
1/3 cup sugar
1/3 cup instant coffee
dash salt
1 teaspoon vanilla extract
2 cups milk, chilled
3/4 cup water
1 cup heavy cream, whipped
unsweetened chocolate, shaved

Beat egg whites with electric mixer until soft peaks form. Gradually beat in sugar until stiff peaks form. In separate bowl, beat egg yolks until lemon colored. Gradually beat coffee, salt, vanilla, milk, and water into egg yolks. Stir in egg-white mixture and whipped cream. Mix well. Serve chilled with chocolate shavings sprinkled over each serving.
Serves 12.

COCOA EGGNOG

1 egg white
1 teaspoon sugar
1 teaspoon cocoa
few grains salt
3/4 cup cold milk

Beat egg white until stiff, then gradually add sugar, cocoa, and salt, beating constantly. Set aside half the mixture. To the rest add cold milk while beating constantly. Pour into a glass, top with remaining egg mixture.
Serves 1.

SEASON'S GREETINGS EGGNOG

2-1/4 cups boiling water
3 tablespoons instant coffee
1 cup sugar
6 eggs, separated
1 quart chocolate ice cream, softened
1 quart milk
1 pint heavy cream
2 teaspoons vanilla extract
1 square (1 ounce) sweet chocolate, shaved
nutmeg

Combine water, coffee, and sugar. Simmer 3 minutes. Chill. Beat egg whites until stiff but not dry.

In separate bowl, beat yolks until thick and lemon colored. Gradually pour in chilled coffee syrup. Beat in ice cream. Stir in milk, heavy cream, and vanilla extract. Fold in egg whites. Pour into punch bowl and serve topped with shaved chocolate and nutmeg.
Serves 25.

Spicy Eggnog

1/2 cup sugar
dash allspice
1/4 teaspoon cinnamon
1/8 teaspoon nutmeg
3 eggs, separated
2 cups milk, chilled
1 cup light cream, chilled
nutmeg

Combine sugar, allspice, cinnamon, and nutmeg. In a separate bowl, beat egg whites with mixer at a high speed until soft peaks form. Gradually beat half of sugar mixture into egg whites until stiff peaks form.

In a small bowl, beat egg yolks until lemon colored. Gradually beat remaining sugar mixture into egg yolks until thick and smooth. Thoroughly fold into whites. Stir in milk and cream. Mix well and chill. Sprinkle with nutmeg.

Serves 12.

Lemonade

As with punch, the secret to good lemonade is to start with a basic sugar syrup that has been boiled for several minutes and to use fresh-squeezed juice. To turn any lemonade recipe into limeade, just substitute lime juice for lemon juice.

Basic Lemonade

6 lemons
2 cups sugar
1 cup water
dash of salt
ice water

Squeeze juice from lemons. Cut rind from 2 lemons into thin strips. In saucepan, boil rinds, sugar, water, and salt, stirring until sugar is dissolved. Cool. Add lemon juice to sugar syrup, cover, and chill well in refrigerator (may be kept in refrigerator for up to a week).

To serve, in each glass mix about 3/4 cup chilled water with 2 tablespoons of lemonade concentrate and crushed ice.

Serves 8.

Frosty Lemonade

1/2 cup sugar
3-1/2 cups water
3/4 cup lemon juice
1 pint lemon sherbet
mint

Combine sugar and 1/2 cup of water in saucepan. Cover and boil 5 minutes, stirring until sugar is dissolved. Chill.

Add lemon juice and remaining 3 cups water. To serve, place about 1/3 cup sherbet in each glass and then fill with lemonade. Garnish with mint.

Serves 6.

Pineapple Lemonade

12-14 lemons
1-1/2 cups sugar
2 quarts water
2 cups crushed pineapple
mint sprigs

Squeeze enough lemons to make 1-1/2 cups of juice. Set aside and cut rind from 2 lemons into pieces. In saucepan, combine lemon rind, sugar, and 1 quart water. Stir over low heat until sugar is dissolved. Boil about 7 minutes. Strain and cool. Add lemon juice, remaining quart of water, and pineapple. Serve over ice in tall glasses and garnish with sprig of mint.

Serves 10.

Fresh Lemonade

3 lemons
3/4 cup sugar
ice cubes
2 cups cold water
maraschino cherries with stems, drained

Thinly slice lemons crosswise. Discard end slices and seeds. Place lemon slices in a large bowl or pitcher. Add sugar. With a wooden spoon or potato masher, pound until sugar is dissolved and slices are broken.

Add 1 tray of ice cubes and water. Stir until very cold.

Pour lemonade, along with lemon slices, into glasses. Garnish with a cherry.

Makes 5 cups or 4 tall glasses.

Pink Lemonade

2 cups sugar
4 cups water
6-7 lemons, juiced
8 strawberries

Boil sugar and water for 10 minutes, then cool. Squeeze lemons to make 2/3 cup fresh lemon juice. Place strawberries in bowl with lemon juice and lightly crush for coloring. Mix all ingredients, chill well, and serve.
Serves 8.

Minted Lemonade

1 bunch mint
1-1/4 cups sugar
1 cup lemon juice
5 cups water

Crush mint leaves (reserve several leaves for garnish), and mix with sugar and lemon juice. Allow to stand 30 minutes in refrigerator. Add water. Strain and pour over ice in glass, and garnish with sprig of mint.
Serves 8.

Pineapple Lemonade for 100

4 cups water
8 cups sugar
8 cups lemon juice
36 ounces pineapple juice concentrate, undiluted
6 oranges, thinly sliced
4 gallons water

Boil water and sugar for 5 minutes, stirring until sugar is dissolved. Cool, then mix with other ingredients. Serve chilled over ice.
Serves 100.

Egg Lemonade

1 egg yolk
3 tablespoons lemon juice, chilled
1-2 tablespoons sugar
1 tablespoon crushed fruit (pineapple or berries)
3/4 cup plain or carbonated water, chilled

Beat egg yolk well. Add other ingredients and beat thoroughly. Serve over ice.
Serves 1.

Pink Lemonade Punch

4 cans frozen lemonade concentrate
8 cups cranberry juice cocktail
1 quart chilled ginger ale
block of ice
1 pint lemon or lime sherbet

Just before serving, prepare lemonade according to label directions. Pour into punch bowl. Add cranberry juice and ginger ale. Mix well. Add ice. Float scoops of sherbet on top.
Serves 50.

Lemonade for 50

2 cups water
4 to 6 cups sugar
2 gallons and 6 cups ice water
4 cups lemon juice (or juice from approximately 2-1/2 dozen lemons)

Boil water and 4 cups of sugar, stirring until sugar is dissolved. Cool, then add ice water and lemon juice. Add additional sugar to taste. Stir until blended.
Serves 50-60.

Tea

Although the Chinese are credited with first using tea as a beverage more than 4,000 years ago, the United States was the first to develop tea bags, iced tea, and instant tea.

Today considered to be the world's most popular drink other than water, tea is made much the same as it always has been—by pouring boiling water over dried leaves of the evergreen tea plant, which grows only in tropical and subtropical climates. Differences between teas are generally due to the processing technique used.

Tea should be stored in a tightly covered container. A dried piece of orange rind kept in the container will add flavor to the tea.

To make traditional black tea, start with a clean china, pottery, or heat-resistant teapot. Scald the teapot with boiling water to heat it before starting the tea. Bring fresh, cold water to a rapid boil before pouring it over the tea leaves. Allow 1 teaspoon of tea (1 tea bag) per cup of water and let steep (soak) for three to five minutes.

Green and oolong teas require lower water temperatures and varying steeping times, depending on the tea.

Strong tea added to any punch helps to harmonize the flavors.

Party Tea

1-1/2 quarts cold water
1/4 pound tea leaves

Make concentrate ahead of time: In a tea kettle, bring cold water to full, rolling boil. Remove from heat. Add loose tea leaves. Stir to immerse leaves. Cover. Let stand 5 minutes. Strain into teapot. Makes about 1 quart.

To serve: Heat a large pot of water to boiling, then remove from heat. Pour 1 to 2 tablespoons concentrate into each teacup. Fill cups with hot water. By varying amount of concentrate, you can vary tea strength.

Serves 50.

Sassafras Tea

sassafras root bark
boiling water
cream
sugar

Steep sassafras root bark, which is obtained in the spring from the sassafras tree, in boiling water for five minutes. To serve, add cream and sugar to taste.

Mint Ice Tea

8 cups boiling water
large bunch of mint
12 tea bags
2 cans frozen lemonade concentrate
1-1/2 cups sugar

In saucepan, pour boiling water over mint and tea bags. Let steep for 15 minutes. Strain.

Add frozen lemon juice and 1-1/4 cups of the sugar. Taste, add remaining sugar as needed to sweeten. Chill well before serving.

Serves 8.

Boston Spiced Fruit Tea

1-1/2 gallons hot, strong tea
1 teaspoon ground cloves
2 teaspoons ground cinnamon
1-1/2 teaspoons nutmeg
1/2 cup lemon juice
1 pint orange juice
1 cup lime juice or frozen limeade
3-1/2 cups sugar, more or less

Mix ingredients well and bring to a boil. Strain through a cloth and serve hot.
Serves 48.

Nutmeg Tea

1 teaspoon butter
1 teaspoon sugar
1/8 teaspoon freshly grated nutmeg
boiling water
cream or milk

Place butter, sugar, and nutmeg in heated mug. Add boiling water until cup is 2/3 full. Stir until butter is melted. Then fill the cup with cream or milk.
Serves 1.

Spiced Tea

7 cups water
6 teaspoons tea
1 stick cinnamon
1 teaspoon whole cloves
1 teaspoon whole allspice
1 orange, juiced
2 lemons, juiced
1 cup sugar

Bring 6 cups water to a boil and steep tea and spices for three minutes.
Strain. Add fruit juices. In separate saucepan, boil sugar and remaining cup of
water for five minutes, stirring until sugar is dissolved. Add to tea and serve
hot or iced.
Serves 12.

Iced Orange Tea

20 cups water
10 oranges
7 lemons
1 cup orange pekoe tea
1 large bunch fresh mint
3 cups sugar

Bring water to a boil in large pan. Meanwhile, squeeze juice from oranges
and lemons, reserving rinds, and strain into a pitcher. Place rinds, tea, and
mint in boiling water. Let stand 1 hour.

Strain tea mixture into pitcher with fruit juices. Add sugar and stir until
sugar is dissolved. Cover and chill. To serve, stir well and pour over ice in
glasses.
Serves 30.

Tea Punch

1 cup sugar
1 cup strong hot tea
1/3 cup lemon juice
3/4 cup orange juice
ice
1 pint ginger ale
1 pint soda water
orange slices

Mix sugar and hot tea, stirring until sugar is dissolved. Add fruit juices. Pour over ice in punch bowl and add ginger ale and soda water. Garnish with slices of oranges.
Serves 12.

Moroccan Mint Tea

1 quart water
4 bags green tea
4 sprigs of mint
1/2 cup sugar

Bring water to a boil. Place tea and mint in teapot, add 2 cups boiling water. Let steep 5 minutes. Add sugar and remaining boiling water, stir. Cover and let steep 5 more minutes. Strain before serving.
Serves 2.

Fruit Tea

9 cups water
9 teaspoons tea
15 whole cloves
2 sticks cinnamon
1-1/3 cup sugar
1 cup orange juice
2/3 cup lemon juice
orange and lemon slices

Bring water to a boil and pour over tea in an earthenware pot. Allow to stand 5 minutes. Strain, add spices and sugar.

When cool, add fruit juices and serve in punch bowl over ice cubes. Garnish with lemon and orange slices.

Serves 12.

Asian Tea

cinnamon stick
4 cups water
4 teaspoons tea
4 sugar cubes
4 slices lemon
cloves

Boil cinnamon stick and water for 3 minutes. Pour over the tea leaves. Steep 5 minutes. To serve, place a sugar cube and clove-studded lemon slice in each cup, then pour tea.

Serves 4.

Hot Spiced Tea

4 cups boiling water
2 tablespoons tea
2/3 cup pineapple juice
1 lemon, juiced
2 oranges, juiced
5 whole cloves
sugar

Make tea. Add fruit juices and cloves, and let simmer about 15 minutes.
Sweeten to taste and serve.
Serves 4-6.

Russian Tea

1/2 gallon water
1 cup sugar
8 whole cloves
8 whole allspice
1 tea ball (or 8 tea bags)
2 lemons, juiced
1 orange, juiced

Boil water, sugar, and spices for 10 minutes. Strain, then add tea and steep
15 minutes. Add fruit juices.
Serves 16.

TENNESSEE BOWL

3 cups cold water
1-1/2 sticks cinnamon (2 inch)
6 whole allspice
6 whole cloves
1-1/2 tablespoons tea
1/2 cup sugar
1/2 cup orange juice
1/4 cup lemon juice
1/4 cup grape juice

Combine water and spices in saucepan. Bring to a bubbling boil and pour over tea leaves. Steep 5 minutes, then strain and add sugar. Stir until the sugar is dissolved. Cover and cool. Add the fruit juices and pour into an ice tray. Freeze until edges begin to harden. Serve in punch cups or small glasses.
Serves 6-8.

HOT TEA PUNCH

1/2 cup sugar
1/2 cup water
1 two-inch stick cinnamon
1 teaspoon lemon rind
1-1/2 teaspoons orange rind
1/4 cup orange juice
2 tablespoons lemon juice
1/4 cup pineapple juice
3 cups boiling water
3 tablespoons tea

Combine sugar, water, cinnamon, lemon rind, and orange rind in a saucepan. Boil 5 minutes. Strain, then add fruit juices. Keep hot. In separate pot, pour boiling water over tea leaves. Steep 5 minutes.

Combine tea and fruit mixture. Serve hot in tea or punch cups.
Serves 6-8.

Iced Tea for 50

2 quarts boiling water
4 tablespoons tea
sugar
4 quarts cold water
2 dozen lemons, juiced
1 dozen oranges, juiced
6 quarts ginger ale

Pour boiling water over tea. Remove from heat. Let stand 2 minutes.
Strain. Sweeten to taste while hot. Add cold water. Add juices and ginger ale
when ready to serve. Add more sugar if necessary.
Serves 50.

Tea House Punch

1/2 cup sugar
1/4 teaspoon nutmeg
1/4 teaspoon allspice
1/4 teaspoon cinnamon
2 cups hot water
3 tea bags
1/4 cup orange juice
1/4 cup lemon juice
2 cups cold water

Combine sugar, spices, and hot water in a saucepan. Boil 1 minute and
pour immediately over the tea bags. Steep 5 minutes. Strain. Mix with fruit
juices and cold water. Serve hot or cold.
Serves 6.

Pineapple Tea Punch

4 tea bags
2 cups water
1/2 cup lemon juice
1 cup pineapple juice
1/2 cup sugar
1/3 cup water

Make double-strength tea by bringing water to a boil and pouring over tea bags. Steep for five minutes. Cool and add fruit juices.

Make sugar syrup by boiling sugar and water together for five minutes, stirring until sugar dissolves.

Add 2-1/2 tablespoons of sugar syrup to tea. Pour over cracked ice. Garnish with fresh mint or sliced lemon.

Serves 3-4.

Mint Tea with Pineapple

5 cups boiling water
5 tea bags
1/2 teaspoon mint flakes
1/4 cup pineapple juice
1/2 cup lemon juice
1/2 cup sugar

Pour boiling water over tea bags and mint flakes in a heated teapot. Cover and steep 6-8 minutes. Strain. Combine with pineapple juice, lemon juice, and sugar. Chill and serve over ice.

Serves 6.

Mint Tea with Orange

2 cups sugar
1/2 cup water
grated rind of 1 orange
6 glasses very strong tea, chilled
6 oranges, juiced
several sprigs of mint
sliced oranges

Boil the sugar, water, and orange rind about 5 minutes. Remove from heat and add the crushed leaves of mint. Let cool.

In pitcher, mix tea and orange juice. To serve, half fill iced tea glasses with crushed ice. Add tea and sweeten to taste with mint syrup. Garnish with a sprig of mint and an orange slice.

Serves 12-15.

Tea and Orange Punch

1 cup water
1 cup sugar
2 cups strong tea
2 cups orange juice
1/2 cup lemon juice
1/2 cup pineapple juice
1/2 cup raspberry syrup from canned fruit
block of ice
1 pint ginger ale
orange slices

Boil water and sugar for 5 minutes, stirring until sugar is dissolved. Remove from heat and chill. Combine tea, fruit juices, raspberry syrup, and sugar syrup. Pour over a block of ice, add ginger ale, and garnish serving bowl with orange slices.

Serves 12.

VEGETABLE *Drinks*

Rich in nutrients and long used as a basis in soups, tomato juice is also delicious and healthy when prepared as a beverage.

Bennington Cooler

1 cup tomato juice
salt and pepper to taste
pinch curry powder
crushed ice

Beat seasonings into well-chilled tomato juice. Pour over crushed ice and serve with a colorful straw. May be topped with 2 tablespoons of ice cold sour cream.
Serves 1.

Hot Veggie Punch

2 cans condensed bouillon and an equal amount of water
5 cups tomato juice
6 or 8 pieces of cut celery (some with tops)
2 small onions, sliced
1 carrot, sliced
sprig of parsley
large bay leaf
7 or 8 whole black peppercorns
juice from 1/4 lemon

Simmer all ingredients except lemon juice. When vegetables are tender, remove from heat. Add lemon juice, strain, and serve. (Can also be served chilled.)
Serves 8.

RECIPE INDEX